THE AWESOME POWER OF
MEDITATION

Defeating Spirit Of Fear And Depression

Luis DeGuzman

Copyright © 2016 by LUIS DEGUZMAN

THE AWESOME POWER OF MEDITATION
Defeating Spirit Of Fear And Depression
by LUIS DEGUZMAN

Printed in the United States of America.

Edited by Xulon Press.

ISBN 9781498463294

All rights reserved solely by the author. The author guarantees all contents are original and do not infringe upon the legal rights of any other person or work. No part of this book may be reproduced in any form without the permission of the author. The views expressed in this book are not necessarily those of the publisher.

www.xulonpress.com

5/17/16

Our Dear Friend Papeng & Mameng,

May all your days on earth be filled with much peace, joy & abundant blessings.

Blessings in Christ,
Bro Tito & Sis Nancie

TABLE OF CONTENTS

DEDICATION vii

I. INTRODUCTION 9
II. WHAT IS MEDITATION? 14
III. UNDERSTANDING THE BIBLE 14
IV. WHY MEDITATE 17
V. UNDERSTANDING THE POWER OF MEDITATION 21
VI. LEARNING TO RESIST THE DEVIL 27
VII. DEFEATING THE SPIRIT OF DEPRESSION, FEAR,
  AND ANXIETY 34
VIII. THE VITAL MINISTRY OF THE HOLY SPIRIT 49
IX. THE CHALLENGE TO STUDY AND MEDITATE 57
X. BECOMING AN OVERCOMER 67

ENDORSEMENTS 99

DEDICATION

To my wife, Nancie, for her encouragement and loving support.

To my children, John, Peter, Lou and his wife Laura,

and Joy and her husband John. To my grandchildren, Remy, Lexi, Asher and Mylee. They all have given me much joy in life.

Also, to all siblings and friends who have been true and kind friends through the years. I'm indebted to them.

I. INTRODUCTION

For as long as I can remember, I have suffered from severe depression, filled with fear, anxiety, and depression. It started at an early age of eight, when I experienced severe bullying, being continuously threatened. Out of nowhere, this neighborhood adult thug came up to me and put his ice pick right on my face. I was so petrified, and I did not know what to do. This merciless bully took pleasure in scaring me and would often point his long ice pick at me. I was immediately paralyzed at the sight of his shining ice pick. This neighborhood thug seemed to be prepared to use the ice pick as his weapon of choice to intimidate helpless children.

This traumatic experience started a lifelong depression and at times became unbearable. Proverbs 17:22 says, "A merry heart doeth good like a medicine; but a broken spirit drieth the bones." My spirit was so broken for so long that I was not able to function normally. Many times, I would not even talk to people. I was always moody and depressed, and I would purposely avoid people. I became overly sensitive and easily upset. I was damaged goods early in life. I have hardly had carefree moments or a joyful existence. Sleep was a welcome respite so I could forget being afraid.

Each morning, I would have the sinking feeling that I would see this dreadful thug again. Many times, people misunderstood me as being snooty, not realizing what I was going through emotionally. When I was a young and impressionable kid, the devil tried to destroy me early in life. However, God turned it around and made my difficult emotional experience help me understand and follow the Word of God closely, to learn to become a strong overcomer later on in life. I was twenty-eight years old when I was led to receive the Lord in my heart and I started a godly Christian walk.

However, my depression continued unabated. I consulted several doctors and psychiatrists, but they could not find a way to cure me. Therefore, I continued to suffer. I would often cry to the Lord to help me. One day, while earnestly praying to the Lord, the Spirit of God led me to 2 Timothy 1:7, which says, "For God hath not given us the spirit of fear; but of power, and of love, and of a sound mind." It immediately made such a big impression on me that I started to meditate on this passage. Somehow, I knew in my spirit that I needed to meditate on this passage continuously. I started whispering and muttering this Bible verse often. I was eager to obey and continuously whispered this passage every chance I could get. I would do it while driving, walking, and cooking—most of the free time I could find.

This started an awesome spiritual journey that I am anxious to share in this book. Thanks be to God that my past ordeal has helped me write this book to guide others who are suffering from a debilitating spirit of fear and depression. It is my prayer that the sound biblical principles I have laid out in this book will help many in the struggles and adversities they face in life. This quest has taught me how to tackle the many problems I have encountered in life and not just against spirit of fear and depression. The Word of God promised to aid us and will do that for us. Acts 19:20 says "... so (they) mightily grew in the Word of God and prevailed."

This book is inundated with so many wonderful Bible verses to aid us in our meditation. We will find much peace, joy and nourishment in our soul, as we embark in knowing, experiencing, and living the precious Word of God. We can never have enough Bible passages planted into our spirit and need to keep planting and planting them into our spirit so that we become strong overcomers. It takes serious commitment and practice of meditation to fortify our spirit. Meditation is that important.

I. Introduction

God's instructions, authority, and power from His words are exclusively for the children of God. First Corinthians 2:14 says, "But the natural man received not the things of the Spirit of God, for they are foolishness unto him; neither can he know them, because they are spiritually discerned." If you wish to experience the spiritual new birth and be a part of God's family, and you would like to partake of this marvelous promise of God, you first need to repent, pray, and receive Jesus Christ into your heart. There is a guide on how to receive the offer of salvation in Christ Jesus in the back portion of this book. If this is your prayerful wish, pray the prayer of repentance and surrender your life to the Lordship of Jesus Christ before proceeding to read this life-changing book.

As you are reading this book, being attentive to it, you will undoubtedly discover many awesome spiritual principles and practices that has been carefully hidden and kept secret by the devil to many believers. These knowledge will greatly help you in your earthly journey, that is often challenging. It will also help you in discovering your true calling in life.

II. WHAT IS MEDITATION?

The word *meditation* has various meanings. The meaning, according to the US National Library of Medicine in the secular world, is a practice in which an individual trains the mind to realize some benefits. This popular belief, practiced by many, is called "transcendental meditation." It involves repeating a "mantra" or saying and whispering the same word or phrase continuously. It is supposed to produce a calming effect. It does, to some degree, give temporary relief because it frees the mind from thinking.

The dictionary (Collin English Dictionary 2012 Digital Edition. William Collins Sons & Co. Ltd. 1979, 1986 @ Harper Collins) describes it as the act of meditating, close or continued thought, turning or revolving a subject in the mind; a serious contemplation, reflecting and musing. The US National Library of Medicine describes meditation as a state of consciousness in which the individual eliminates environmental stimuli from awareness so that the mind can focus on a single thing, producing a state of relaxation and relief from stress. A wide variety of techniques is used to clear the mind of stressful inside and outside interferences. It includes meditation therapy.

To the Hindu mind, in the West, meditation (Meditation—Origin of Buddhist Meditation by Alexander Wynne. 2007/ ISBN 0–415–42387–2 page 4) means a concentrated state of mind in serious reflection. The Latin root of the word meditation, *medici* means to heal, an effort to heal afflictions of the mind, the hurt ego, by trying

II. What Is Meditation?

to understand the cause of the problem and finding a way to solve it, that is, by knowing what counter measures to take. To meditate thus, is to deepen a state of understanding. In the East, however, meditation does not mean thinking at all, but fixing the mind to a spiritual ideal, to be one with, or thought process dissolving the consciousness of it. In short, it is a spiritual renewal on the feeling of oneness, with a higher source of life.

However, the thrust of this book is to illustrate meditation using biblical principles, and teaching how this works. It is also to shed light to the godly ways of meditation and its effect on believers. Some people question whether it really works. This study will show us how effective godly meditation is when it is properly practiced and applied. We can also be confident that it is so because the Lord God made it a commandment to meditate on His Word. Psalm 119:97 says, "O how I love thy law! it is my meditation all the day." Most believers are not practicing meditation very much, and many believers do not fully understand the need for it. Why is there a need to meditate? Why not just read the Bible? These are common questions by believers whenever the subject of meditation is brought up.

III. UNDERSTANDING THE BIBLE

The Bible is our very precious inheritance from our Lord God. He reveals Himself through His Word. God breathes on His Word, making it to be alive for us. John 6:63 says," The Words that I speak unto you are alive and have spirit." The Bible is not just another book that we casually read. The author of the Bible is God Himself, and we need to carefully study and absorb it. Psalm 138:2 says, "Thou has magnified thy Word above your name." God made this startling statement to remind us how important is the Word of God. Matthew 24:35 says, "Heaven and earth shall pass away, but my words shall not pass away." The Bible is full of power, guidance, and revelations that we need to learn and discover.

The Bible is truly a magnificent book. It was written in the span of 1,600 years with many authors in truly amazing harmony. No other book can make that claim. Most books written become obsolete after a few years, but the Bible becomes more relevant with each passing year. The Bible prophecies are so accurate that only a Supreme Being could foretell them. There are over 300 prophecies in the Old Testament of the coming of the Lord Jesus Christ alone. The staggering prophecies concerning Israel is so accurate that it is truly mind boggling.

Many skeptics have tried to discredit the Bible through the centuries but to no avail. The Bible remains the bestselling book in the world each year. A noted mathematician (Professor Peter W. Stoner. Science Speaks. 1957 Moody Press) calculated that if just eight major

III. Understanding The Bible

prophecies were fulfilled, out of several hundred prophecies, the odds of it happening is so staggering that it would require a calculation up to the 24th power. It simply means that all Bible prophecies coming to pass is not possible without the divine intervention of the God of the universe.

One awesome prophecy written in Zechariah 9:9, predicted the coming of the Messiah 400 years before it happened. It predicted the exact day that the promised Messiah would come to Jerusalem in a triumphant entry, riding on a donkey. It happened accurately as prophesied, and only Jesus Christ was able to fulfill that prophecy. Another odd-defying prophecy was the return of the Jewish people to Palestine to form a nation. Against all odds, Israel became a nation. The United Nation unanimously voted to make Israel as a sovereign nation on May 9, 1948. (Prophecy Fulfilled: Israel becomes a nation in 1948. Prophecy Society of Atlanta)

The Bible, in spite of so many militant critics, survived the test of time. It remains the most important and relevant manuscript ever written. The Bible has proven itself to be the holy manuscript, even after numerous attempts to destroy it. In spite of all efforts, it remains the indestructible Holy Word of God. If a person is determined to know the existence of God, all he needs to do is examine the claims of the Bible. After examining the Bible honestly, one has to arrive to an unmistakable conclusion that God is in heaven. It would take more faith to believe that there is no God, after carefully examining the accurate prophecies in the Bible, than to believe there is. It would be so reckless for anyone to deny the inerrancy of the Bible with such overwhelming proof. After verifying the claims of the Bible, a person cannot just say, "I don't believe there is God." This is like saying, "I don't believe there is such a country called Egypt because I have not seen it."

The Bible declares accurately that certain people do not want to believe the truth and submit to the teachings of Christ because their deeds are evil. By accepting the teachings of Christ, it would be an admittance of their guilt. The evidence of the existence of God is true and accurate as seen by closely examining the holy Bible. The immutability of the Bible clearly shows in the study of fulfilled prophecies. However, no amount of solid evidence would suffice and convince unbelievers and biased observers. The Bible declares in Psalm 14:1, "The fool hath said in his heart, there is no God." A person must have a repentant heart to approach the holy and Living God. The Lord God solemnly promised that we will find Him if we seek Him with all our heart.

Men are desperate to find peace, and they will never have it apart from a real relationship with the Prince of Peace, Jesus Christ, the Son of the Living God. Why is it so hard to study the Bible for some people? It is because the prince of this world, the devil, has darkened their mind.

It is fundamental for us, believers, to learn the Bible well and master it to grow as strong believers. Great athletes develop their talents by learning the basic knowledge of their game. It would be difficult to excel in any game without first knowing the fundamentals of the game. Coaches, who coach top college teams in the country, put heavy emphasis in drilling their players to learn the fundamentals. The fundamental understanding of the Bible is important for us to grow in the Lord. We need to study the Bible to be convinced of the inerrancy of the holy Bible.

IV. WHY MEDITATE

Why is our meditation so important? It is like planting seeds into good soil and watering it often. If we want our plants to grow, we must continue to care for it. As we keep watering the plants we have planted, we would soon see them grow. First, we see the blade, then the leaves, and then tiny branches. The little pine seed we have planted into a good soil will grow into a big pine tree: tall, majestic, and full of heavy branches and needles. However, the process takes time, and it will be a long time before a pine seed becomes a tall towering tree.

It would be foolish for a farmer to plant seeds and just leave them alone without caring for them. There are diligent farmers and lazy farmers, and their harvest will depend on the amount of time they put into cultivating and watering their plants. In many produce markets, fruits, nuts, and vegetables are graded according to their size and quality. There is more to it than just planting seeds. Good farmers watch over their plants carefully.

Another good example we can use are soldiers going to war. The prince of this world, the devil, wants to defeat us and neutralize us in every encounter. As soldiers of Christ, we need to be well trained and combat ready because we do not know when the devil and his demons may choose to strike and mount an attack against us. Our enemy, the devil, is no ordinary adversary, and he is a seasoned warrior. He has been around for a very long time and knows how to fight. He is very deceptive and skillful in injecting wicked and negative thoughts into our minds. He would send to us negative thoughts that would appear to be real problems for us. He will blow our problems out of proportion, making them appear to be unsurmountable. He is the father of all lies, and he will continue to lie to us.

Our study and meditation of the Word is not something we do for a season and expect great results. Like a young plant, our spirits need constant watering with the Word of God. It is the food of our spirit. First Peter 2:2 says, "As newborn babes, desire the sincere milk of the word, that he may grow thereby." Our spirits need to be nourished by the Word of God daily in order for them to grow vigorous and healthy. God is fully aware of the difficult challenges we go through in life, considering how the devil and evil men make things very difficult for us. Willfully and carelessly ignoring God's instructions laid out in the Bible puts us in great peril. There are clear warnings from the Bible that we need to carefully observe. Its instructions are clear warnings to protect us against the wiles of the devil. Those are red flags, which should not be ignored.

In this world, it will serve us well if we are alert and fully aware that we are in deep spiritual conflicts with the devil. The devil is relentless and opposes anything godly. Wicked spirits want to get inside us, but they have been stripped of spiritual power. First Corinthians 10:5 says, "... we should refute arguments and theories and reasoning and every lofty thing that set itself against the knowledge of God." The devil has no legal right to bring fear into our life. We must refuse anything that the devil sends to our mind. We are to be very selective in what we accept to believe. We have to listen only to words that clearly line up with God's Word. Listening too much to the news media must be minimized as it focuses on bad news.

Most significant things we do in life take time, whether studying in school, building a career, or establishing a good relationship. The long period of time is needed to help us reach our goal in life. The time we spend in pursuing our aim in life help us mature greatly. Olympic gymnasts spend around six to eight hours daily to perfect their routine and excel in their sport. It is sad to see men devote so much time in their worldly pursuit that has no real permanent value.

IV. Why Meditate

Many of their seemingly great accomplishments are soon forgotten as other athletes eclipse their records of accomplishments.

Communion with God through prayers and meditation means emptying ourselves to God and allowing God to reveal Himself to us. It is an awesome privilege for us to be able to pray to our Father, the God who rules the entire universe. Not everyone can approach God; only those who have experienced the New Birth in Christ can come to God.

The Bible spells out our holy covenant with God. It is a legal and binding contract, and it stipulate the provisions written in the contract. It tells us our rights and privileges as followers of Christ. It tells us the full extent and scope of our authority as being members of the body of Christ. Jesus Christ is the vine, and we are the branches. We need to abide in Christ, or we will wither away. Studying and meditating on the Word of God help us to be strongly abiding in Him. Jesus said to abide in Him for apart from Him, we cannot do anything. We are totally helpless without Him. As we abide in Him, we also abide in His love. We cannot possibly abide in Christ without studying, praying, and meditating.

What then is the study and proper meditation of the Word? Studying the Word will not profit us if we just read the Bible without carefully studying its godly instructions. Being aware that we are studying the holy Word of God, grasping it and being mindful of it, will help us in our study of the Bible. By studying and meditating on the Word of God, we are planting and transferring precious seeds into our spirits. Our faith keeps growing as we maintain our study and meditation of the Word of God.

The spirit of man, the real us, is neutral and can be trained for either good or bad. Criminals have trained their spirit to be bad, and they commit all kinds of criminal activities. They have conditioned their spirits to be tough and have allowed their fellow criminals to train them. It is why we need to train our spirits with the Word of God on a daily basis to continue to conform to the mind of Christ. Our commitment to study and meditate on the Word of God far outweigh the sacrifices and hard work we put into it. God will always be gracious when we humble ourselves before Him and come to a place of brokenness of spirit.

We must learn to forget those things in the past, whether failures or successes. Rather, we should press forward toward the mark for the prize of the high calling of God in Christ Jesus. We can be a living branch of the living vine, Christ Jesus. It is our privilege as a child of God. The secret of perfect peace is to learn how to carry our burden and to let go when it gets too heavy, trusting the Lord to carry it for us. Our daily meditation will help us discover the many blessings available to us.

V. UNDERSTANDING THE POWER OF MEDITATION

Let us examine how the apostles grew in their faith in Christ. They started to grow by remembering what they have seen and heard from the Lord. We retain things in our memory by thinking and dwelling on it often. The apostles kept dwelling on the teachings of Christ often and it became the basis of their unshakeable faith, even to the point of death and boldly defending their faith in the living Christ.

Oftentimes, believers keep dwelling on their difficult circumstances and not on the precious promises of God's Word. They have been neglectful and have allowed their minds to stray on their difficult circumstances. The Word of God has become dormant in their daily existence. The Word of God is like a precious seed that needs to be planted into our spirits and watered on a regular basis in order to grow. Planted on a good soil and carefully watered and cared for, the seed, or the Word of God, grows to be lush and fruitful.

Of all of the many commandments of God, the instruction to meditate on His Word is one of the important instructions for us believers to follow. This message has to be embedded in our mind. If meditation is very important, should we not take every opportunity to study and meditate on God's Word? If we believe this to be true, we should take advantage to meditate on the precious Word of God at every opportunity.

We read in the book of Joshua, chapter 10, how Joshua was able to grow so strong in faith that he was able to stop the sun and the moon from moving for one day. In their fierce battle against the Amorites, the Israelites needed more daylight to defeat the enemy, and Joshua commanded the sun and the moon to stop. Imagine being able to stop the sun and the moon from moving for one day. It is truly incredible what faith can do. Many believers think that when God said if you have faith, you can move mountains, it was merely a figure of speech. Joshua proved otherwise that he was able to command the gigantic sun and the moon to stop at his command. His commitment on meditating on the Word of God gave him unwavering faith. Even the sun and the moon had to obey unshakeable faith of Joshua. How would we like to have the same kind of faith?

The Sequoia trees in Redwood Forest in Northern California are over 200 years old. Their trunks measure up to twenty-five feet in diameter. That is so huge that a large hole was cut through one of the trees, allowing cars to pass through it. Its deep roots allow it to stand very tall. It is a testament of how strong those majestic Sequoia trees are. Heavy snow in winter and strong winds have failed to bring down those mighty trees. Similarly, when our spirits are firmly anchored on the Word of God through our constant study and meditation, we become like those Sequoia trees that could withstand the strong fierce winds of trials and testing in life.

The Word of God has many benefits for us. It acts as our guide and strong protection in life. Psalm 119:105 says, "Thy Word is a lamp unto my feet, and a light unto my path." The Lord knows the power of His Word and uses it effectively against the devil. The Lord decisively defeated the devil in the wilderness. The devil tempted him three times, and each time the Lord used the Word to defeat him. The Lord wants to encourage us to learn from His example and learn to have faith in His Word. Jesus said in Matthew 24:35, "Heaven and earth shall pass away, but my Words shall not pass away." The Word of God will remain forever.

What does it take to grow strong in our faith? The word is *passion*. We need to have passion to study and meditate on the Word of God. Casual study and meditation of the Word of God won't cut

V. Understanding The Power Of Meditation

it. Our study and meditation must become a way of life. Like Joshua, we need to study and meditate on the Word of God at every chance we can find in each day. One of the most important reasons why we need to meditate on Bible passages is it will come back to our remembrance in time of real need.

Developing a habit to do physical exercise or spiritual meditation does not come easy for us. It is necessary to reinforce a daily routine to have deep effect on us in becoming a strong overcomer. We see world-class gymnasts execute the same number of routines each day to become flawless in their execution. We marvel at the agility and balance in their athletic performances. What we do not get to see are their many hours of practice in the gym each day to perfect their routines.

Like a seed that needs to be planted before it can grow, so is the Word of God. It must first be planted into our spirit. The Word of God is our great gift from God. It is our guide on how to live victoriously in this treacherous and evil world. The Word of God has specific instructions that pertain to life and godliness. It holds tremendous power to assist us in whatever adversities we will face in life. God puts supreme value on His Word. It is truly our great inheritance from God.

The power of God was not for the privileged few among the first-century Christians but for all those who believe. Psalm 37:3 says, "Trust in the Lord, and do good, so shall thou dwell in the land, and verily thou shalt be fed." The Lion of Judah, our Lord Jesus Christ, shall break every chain. God's Word is from everlasting to everlasting. His Word cannot fail. God's Word is true, and when we rest on this truth, mighty results will follow. God promised it. Perfect love will never want to have the preeminence in everything. It will always be willing to take the back seat. If we seek nothing but the will of God, He will always put us in the right place at the right time.

There is nothing more thrilling than a life that is illuminated each day with the Word of God. Psalm 119:130 says, "The entrance of the Word giveth light and give understanding to the simple." Our Father reveals Himself to us through His Word, and He will give us profound satisfaction as we hunger for His Word. Psalm 107:9 says, "For He satisfy the longing soul." The Bible is our heavenly bank account. When we learn to meditate on the Word of God, we can draw from it. We are putting massive spiritual deposits into our spirit as we continue to meditate.

By faith, we activate the Word of God. Faith is the key to access the power of God's Word. Faith is the victory. If we believe, it is ours, but we can only believe and rest on the Word of God when we continuously meditate on it. The Holy Spirit is grieved when we know these things but don't exploit and appropriate it. Daniel 11:32, says "But people who know their God shall prove themselves strong and do great exploits." Will we not believe God so that He can bring us to the manifestation of His power?

The bridge between the seen and the unseen, the natural realm and the spiritual realm, is the Word of God. We must have the continual quality quiet time with the Lord and fellowship with Him, being mindful of His words. This is the foundation of deep inner peace. Deep inner peace comes from spending quiet time with the Lord. Ample time spent alone with God brings us closer to Him. Philippians 3:8 says, "I count all things loss for the excellency of the knowledge of Christ Jesus, my Lord ..."

If we love our Lord, we want to spend a lot of time with Him. Psalm 119:165 says, "Great peace have they which love thy law." As we do our best to abide in the love of God and dwell in His love, we will find that it is much easier to love other people and even those who are difficult to love. We will soar like giant eagles as we learn to surrender each day to the Holy Spirit, trusting totally in His power to lift us high above the problems that seem so difficult to us, with our many human limitations. Proverbs 23:26 says, "My son, give me thy heart and let thy eyes observe my ways." The Lord's deep inner peace is only available when we empty out our hurried and confused selves each day, along with the world's incessant demands. Jesus gave us His peace, and He wants us to be quiet and confident in the midst of trials and tribulations. Learning to trust God will bring us godly peace that is so elusive to many.

V. Understanding The Power Of Meditation

Wisdom and understanding will give us everything the world craves. They will lead to peace more valuable than the riches that many people anxiously look for. The world searches for fame, riches, and fortune, but better things are available to those who find wisdom and understanding. Proverbs 3:13 says, "Happy is the man that finds wisdom and the man that gains understanding."

If we are definitely with the Lord, we will never go away disappointed. All things are possible if we will only believe. He will meet us in our absolute hopelessness. As He is, so are we in his world. Nothing is too hard for our Lord. The Word of God is sufficient today. If we will only dare to believe God's Word, we will see the performance of His Word that will truly be wonderful. Matthew 11:28 says, "Come unto me, all ye that labor and are heavy laden and I will give you rest."

We will do more in one year if we are filled with the Spirit of God than we could do in fifty years apart from His Spirit. The secret of great men of God is they continuously wait upon the Lord. He will guide and satisfy us with long lives and show us His salvation. In His presence, there is fullness of joy, and at His right hand, there is pleasure forevermore. There are so many nuggets to be found in the Word of God as we keep digging at it. Men will never find peace and joy apart from the counsel of the Word of God. It will help many believers to find victory if they will understand this simple instruction.

Lots of believers read their Bible occasionally but remain spiritually weak. It is because the Word of God has to be planted through daily meditation before it can become our great inheritance and possession. This statement is often repeated in this book for strong emphasis.

We can get things from God only in the line of living faith. God never fails. God can never fail. Realize what would happen if we believed God's Word. The Bible is full of invitations for us to come and partake His grace, His power, and His righteousness. Spirit-filled Christians are full of joy and peace. They just "bubble over." Psalm

25:14 says, "The secret of the Lord is with them that fear Him and He will show them His covenant."

We realize God's promise of many blessings and breakthrough in our lives when we continue to meditate on His Word. However, God does not give blessings that He has promised until we show careful responsible action to receive the promises of God. No one should expect to be prosperous and blessed until he starts doing what the Word of God says. Many people want the fulfillment of God's promises immediately without first taking responsible action on their part. Worthwhile pursuit takes time, and it needs to develop. God has a different timetable than our schedule. None of us will ever gain anything truly worthwhile in just an instant. Any truly worthwhile pursuit takes time to develop. We cannot expect God's answers to leap to our schedule. Remember, God's marvelous answers will happen when we put His Word into action. Just as an apple tree takes time to grow and bear fruits, so our patient pursuit of His promises, when we learn to wait for the Word of God to mature in our spirit.

If we spend time with our Master, we will fill up our reservoir with spiritual power we need to serve Him and maintain our inner peace. It is flesh versus spirit. We are to be moved only through God's Word. Our feelings and emotions often run counter to the Word of God. We are to be careful not to allow our feelings and emotion overrule the Word of God. Nothing can be compared with the precious time of enlightenment when God reveals more of His great wisdom. Psalm 71:1 says, "In Thee O Lord do I put my trust, let me never be put into confusion."

We must consider each day as a loss when we fail to pray, study, and meditate on the precious Word of God. It takes just fifteen to thirty minutes to study one chapter of the Bible each day. Romans12:2 says, "Be ye transformed by the renewing of your mind, that ye may prove what is good, and acceptable, and perfect, will of God."

VI. LEARNING TO RESIST THE DEVIL

The devil will fight hard to prevent us from having strong faith. The devil does not want the seed to start rooting and getting the chance to grow. We read in Mark 4:15 how the devil steals the Word from being planted into man's spirit so no fruit can be produced. It is why some men are not interested with the gospel and avoid further talk of it.

If the heart of man is hard, thorny, and rocky, the Word of God will not have a chance to grow and bear fruit. Oftentimes, we limit the power of God in our lives because of our limited understanding of the Word of God. At times, we think that we have seemingly strong faith until we encounter difficult problems in life and our faith starts to wobble. Why? That is because the Word is not fully established and secured in our spirits. The Word of God having no roots in our spirits cannot help us when the heavy storms and persecution comes.

Doubts, fear, and unbelief are strong spirits that undermine our faith. Like a house, if we do not build the foundation of our faith upon the solid rock, faith in Jesus Christ and His Word, when heavy rain comes, our house will be washed away. The Lord means every Word He has promised us. However, we can only activate it through our faith. When we have inactive and weak faith due to ignorance or neglect, the Word of God will not be able to help us for lack of faith to believe it. Additionally, we will greatly exacerbate our weak position if we think that the devil is not a dangerous enemy and is not full of wicked mischief to undermine us.

Satan has darkened the minds of multitude of people to believe and receive the truth. The devil's top priority is to twist the truth of the Bible and to keep people away from the Holy Bible. The devil has created many forms of religion to worship false gods. Many cults keep sprouting around the world. Their followers are so militant in their false belief. The devil is a master deceiver and very cunning in misleading people what to believe. The devil has enslaved the cult members in that they make their good work as their basis for going to heaven. They base their salvation on their own merit and twisting the truth on the redemptive finished work of Christ. We should not be surprised why multitudes will not accept the teachings of Christ. Even the Lord Jesus Christ taught in parables to hide the truth from those unbelievers who refuse to believe the truth.

Many times in life, we are defeated for allowing the devil to buffet us for lack of understanding of all the spiritual authority available to us. Hosea 4:6 says, "My people perish for lack of knowledge." Negative thoughts and emotion should not be entertained; instead we must keep focusing on the Word of God by continuously meditating on it. The attacks of the devil are relentless, and we must resist them strongly through the Word of God.

When the fierce attacks of the devil come, we must act at once and be ready to do battle by immediately releasing what Ephesians 6:17 calls "the sword of the Spirit, the Word of God." The devil must be fully convinced that we won't quit meditating and releasing our mighty weapons continuously to force him to retreat and flee. When the devil is quiet, it doesn't mean he is dormant. He is just waiting for an opening. We just need to be ready to repel any of his wicked attacks.

When thinking of fighting those wicked demons that are torturing our mind, try to picture the great invasion of the Allied forces of occupied Europe in 1944. The Allied forces fought their way into the heavily defended positions of the fanatical German soldiers in many cities and towns. It was a real struggle for the Allied soldiers in liberating Europe. It took real courage to fight the fiercely resisting Germans from house to house and street to street in savage armed conflicts that at times became bloody hand-to-hand combat. The

VI. Learning To Resist The Devil

Germans did not quit easily. Likewise, in spiritual combat, we must not expect the devil and his demons to quit easily, either, and our victory has to be won.

Believers who are fortified with the Word of God will not be attacked by the devil often. The devil comes from time to time just to see if we are still formidable and rooted in the Word of God. It is important to keep remembering that the battlefield is in our mind. The devil can capture our mind if we keep receiving and dwelling on barrages of negative thoughts. The devil is persistent and won't quit easily. We must resist all negative thoughts at once.

The devil has decisively captured the minds of many, and some are so fearful that they do not even want to be alone or to leave their homes. Being in dark places terrify and greatly overwhelm them. There are all kinds of fear that the devil sends to mankind. Many of his victims are either in the cemetery, in jail, or in mental hospitals. The devil also has unquenchable desire to inflict pain and suffering on mankind. He wants us totally annihilated and vanquished.

Just knowing that those wicked spirits that are throwing fiery darts at our mind can be stopped gives us real advantage. The devil and his cohorts are masters of deception. They do not want us to know that they are sowing negative thoughts into our mind. They make it appear as if it is just our mind thinking of those fearful and depressing thoughts. Fear of rejection is one strong weapons of the devil uses because people mistakenly look for people for their source of approval. The devil can block that channel to cause us to feel less worthy. However, the devil cannot block the channel coming from the Lord as we reach out to Him.

If we keenly observe how those wicked spirits attack, we would see that they send wicked and fearful thoughts from out of nowhere. Many times, we are not even thinking of any negative thought, and it would suddenly be dropped into our mind without any warning. Those evil spirits employ various strategies to defeat us. They will keep sending wicked thoughts to see which one we would receive and entertain. The devil is always fishing with many lines to see which one we would bite. Once we are caught in his fishing line, the devil sends reinforcements for more evil spirits to increase their attacks.

The devil has an army, and it is well organized. Each demon has his own field of expertise. Some would be in the field of vindictiveness, hate, and anger. Some are in the field of sensuality, lust, and pornography. Others are in the field of depression, self-pity, worry, and anxiety. Others are in the field of haughtiness, greed, treachery, and gossip. Some are in the field of insecurity and self-condemnation. Others are in drugs, drunkenness, and many more.

They are so well organized, and each one is assigned a specific job to undermine us. Fear is one of the biggest weapons the devil uses against mankind. Fear runs the whole world's system. We hardly read any good news in newspapers or hear from TV and radio. The daily news report is mostly bad news. News reporters are conditioned to put emphasis on bad news. If you notice, even when the economy is doing well, business news reporters would often mention possible economic downtrends. Many traders in the stock market made fortunes by capitalizing on bad news and investing heavily on the downtrend of stocks.

The devil came to kill, steal and destroy as we read in John 10:10. He and his demons would do everything in their power to cause constant havoc and calamities around the world. The devil makes a habit of stealing the Word of God and putting up heavy opposition against us when we commit ourselves to the study and meditation of the Word of God.

Many times, believers who initially try to start reading and meditating on the Word of God find themselves sleepy and often distracted. The devil has only one plan for mankind, and it is to kill, steal, and destroy. Knowing full well the wicked intentions of the devil, it would make great sense for us to study the Bible, learning how to resist against the devil and his demons.

From the beginning of time, the devil has focused on undermining the works of God. The clever temptation of the devil to lure Adam and Eve to disobey God by eating the forbidden fruit was all

VI. Learning To Resist The Devil

too clear. The devil is a master deceiver and successfully deceived Adam and Eve to submission to him by eating the forbidden fruit. The devil showed his cunning by making Adam and Eve believe his lies. The devil lied and promised that Eve and Adam would be like God once they ate the forbidden fruit. The high treason committed by Adam and Eve made them sinners, and they were vanished from paradise. The curse entered the world and has been in operation ever since. Adam, due to his disobedience, legally surrendered the ownership of the world to the devil. The world has become a mess as a result of being ruled by Satan.

However, the good news is, our Lord and Savior Jesus Christ paid the ultimate sacrifice and defeated Satan at the Cross. Jesus paid the sins of mankind, and Satan lost ownership of the world. He no longer rules the world with an iron grip, but he now uses lies, intimidation, and cunning to deceive unsuspecting mankind.

When we are facing our wicked enemies, we had better be sure we're fully convinced of our authority and the superiority of our weapons. It is going to be a decisive battle, and the devil and his demons will fight. They will stay in the trenches until they are sure we will not retreat and will continue firing our state-of-the-art weaponry, our precision guided missile, which is the Word of God.

As fierce and skillful the devil and his demons are, they are no match to the sword of the Spirit, the living Word of God. If we refuse to be intimidated and learn to resist the heavy pressure coming from the devil, we will come out victorious with each encounter. The devil must be convinced that he cannot outwit or outlast us. It is important to remember that the devil will fight us to make us think that our resistance is futile; but we need to keep it up. Our focus in staying on the Word of God through meditation will do the job.

We could always count on the Word of God to defeat the devil. We always need to remember that the devil is no match against the powerful Word of God. In this world, we will encounter trials and difficult challenges; but Jesus said in John 16:33, "ye shall have tribulation; but be of good cheer, I have overcome the world." Those trials and tribulations should not overwhelm us when we are walking in faith. On some occasions, God will send trials into our life to build up our spiritual muscles and to see if we truly love Him. We read this in 1 Thessalonians 2:4 "... but God which tried our hearts ..."

We are in a vicious fight with the devil and his demons, and we will be in a spiritual conflict whether we like it or not. We need to learn how to sense when the devil is sending fiery darts into our minds. The devil will drop those negative thoughts on us when we least expected it; many times it is when we are tired, angry, discouraged, and hungry. We will be susceptible to his attacks if we do not realize that evil thoughts are being sent to our mind. The devil is always probing our mind for weaknesses.

The attacks of the devil come in progression. First, a thought comes, then it becomes an imagination when we entertain it, and finally it becomes a stronghold. It is very hard to dislodge a stronghold, and our fight will be prolonged if it is prolonged. Like preparing for battle, we need to be sure that we are well prepared for a sustained battle. Many battles have been lost due to negligence and lack of preparation.

We are facing a formidable enemy, who is skillful and treacherous and must not be underestimated. The devil employs different tactics to try to destroy us. He and his minions have prepared well and have studied their target meticulously, learning our strengths and weaknesses. He has studied the terrain of the battlefield to gain an advantage. They are fixed in their goal to destroy us, to accomplish total annihilation if it is at all possible. If the devil can sow real doubts and unbelief into our mind about the existence of God, he has won a great victory.

The devil and his wicked spirits have been keenly observing us, monitoring our ways to find weaknesses and points of entry. It has been said that the devil's greatest weapon is to make mankind believe that he doesn't exist. The world is clueless of the wicked and sinister plans of the devil for mankind. It is not surprising why so many colleges even use the devil as their mascot. They call him by many names like Blue Devil, Diablos, Red Devil and other names.

VI. Learning To Resist The Devil

The Lord has put a force within us whereby we can defeat the devil decisively. However, the moment we fall into sin, divine life ceases to flow, and our life becomes one of helplessness. At this stage, we are no match against the devil, and we need to cry to the Lord and ask for forgiveness. We are never to rely on human plans, but we should seek clear guidance through the Word of God.

Temptations will come to all of us while we are living in this world. If we are not worth tempting, we are not worth much in the Kingdom of God. It is a blessed thing to learn that God's Word can never fail. Second Corinthians 5:7 says, "We walk by faith and not by sight."

The devil is on a rampage in this end times. The devil induces men to beat their wives, parents to hurt their children, children to become abusive toward their parents, and men to kill other men. It is the devil making them lose their mind and give in to hatred and violence. We must train our mind not to entertain wicked thoughts coming from the devil and his demons. James 4:7 says, "Submit yourselves therefore to God. Resist the devil, and he will flee from you." We resist him by the all-powerful Word of God.

The devil will meet us at every turn, but the Spirit of God will always lift up a standard against him. All we need to do is keep releasing the Word of God through our meditation. The Lord will always honor His Word when we fully embraced it by faith. We must be careful what we allow into our mind. The devil sends worries to us. Let us remember that worry is suicide in an installment plan. It robs us of the joy of living.

The Word of God is our legally binding covenant with God. We will have missed out in God's many opportunities and blessings by not studying and meditating in His precious Word. There are many blessings available to us through God's Word. It drives the devil crazy when we meditate on the Word of God continuously. There are heavy tremors and panic in the camp of the devil and his demons when we start to commit to study, pray, and meditate.

VII. DEFEATING THE SPIRIT OF DEPRESSION, FEAR, AND ANXIETY

Have you ever met anyone who has not experienced some form of depression, fear, or anxiety in life? We all have experienced being victims of those malevolent spirits. Spirits of depression, fear, and anxiety are strong, wicked spirits that are persistent and constantly harassing us. Believers who have not been taught how to resist the devil have allowed the spirits of depression, fear, and anxiety to harass their mind. Uninformed believers have stayed and have dwelt on the wicked lies of the devil, often entertaining the feeling of hopelessness and fear. They have allowed their minds time after time to dwell on difficult problems and not on the Word of God to help them.

Spirits of depression, fear, and anxiety affect millions. Not so long ago, famous actor Robin Williams committed suicide due to severe depression. Many celebrities and rich people end their lives rather than go through life with depression. Depression saps the very life from us. A person afflicted with depression cannot function properly. The joy of living ceases to exist. Depression is like a faucet of water that keeps dripping without end. The devil keeps sending debilitating thoughts that have affected millions of people. It has been estimated that over 40 million Americans are suffering from some form of depression. The medical treatment for depression is costing the United States $42 billion a year. Many who have severe depression

VII. Defeating The Spirit Of Depression, Fear, And Anxiety

have become suicidal. The antidepressant drugs have become big business; drug companies make billions of dollars on them each year.

The thoughts we feed on and allow to enter our mind is what will become of our mindset. Studies of sociologists reveal that hardened criminals developed their evil mindset by constantly hanging around with other criminals. They feed on each other's criminal thoughts and activities. Influence of friends and loved ones contributes to our character and personality development. Students group together according to their personality make-up in school. We cannot underestimate the influence of other people in our lives.

Influence of television, magazines, radio, books, newspapers, and movies greatly contribute to our way of thinking, beliefs, and conviction. We should never give way to human opinions but yield only to God's Word. How can we do that? It is done through His Name, through faith in His Name, through faith He gives us, and through faith in His living Word.

Forget everything except what God has said about Jesus. There is nothing that our great God cannot do. He will do everything for us if we will dare to believe His Word. Today, there is bread, there is life, and there is health in every child of God through His powerful Word. If we truly believe that everything is working for good to them that love God, then we should simply relax and trust God.

Faith versus Fear
Love versus Hate
Trust versus Panic
Confident versus Nervousness
Fearless versus Fearful
Settled versus Uneasiness
Kind versus Merciless
Peace versus Worry
Joy versus Chaos

The expression "Let go and let God" should be in our vocabulary. God will take care of everything if we just let go and let Him deal with our troubles. Pride and unbelief will stop us from entering into the rest of God, which we can enter through humility and trust. Our Lord releases His great power to those who are calm, trusting, and faithful toward Him. His peace is our peace. His wisdom is our wisdom; His strength is our strength. Our Lord can handle anything.

If we dare trust our wonderful Lord and embrace His Word, the Lord of life will be more than sufficient for all our needs. If we dare trust Him, He will never fail us. God says that the prayer of faith shall raise the sick. The Lord shall raise the sick when we meet the conditions. The Bible declares that perfect love cast out fear. If we truly believe that God loves us unconditionally, what is there to fear? Fear cannot exist in the presence of God. We can multiply His grace and peace by constantly drawing closer and closer to Him. Confusion in our lives comes to the degree that we operate apart from the Holy Spirit. Peace comes to the degree we are one with the Great One who lives inside us. There is no way that fear can get to us if our love is perfect.

Oh, if we would only believe God! Some men have never tasted and enjoyed the grace and peace of God. Unbelief rob us of so much blessings from God. Satan is always trying to bring saints into disrepute; but the Holy Spirit is always on hand to help us in the season of trials, temptation, and testing. Job said, "When He has tried me, I shall come forth as gold."

The devil wants to capture our minds because the battle is in the mind. Continuous meditation is the key to defeating the spirit of depression, fear, and anxiety. As we continually whisper and mutter the Word of God, we are able to dislodge the negative thoughts that the devil keeps trying to implant into our mind.

Whenever an evil spirit is attacking us, rebuke and resist him through the Word of God. When we find ourselves constantly harassed with negative thoughts, we need to remember the instruction of the Lord to *switch* our thinking into positive. It tells us how to do it in Philippians 4:8, "Finally brethren, whatsoever things are true, whatsoever things are honest, whatsoever things are just, whatsoever things are lovely, whatsoever things are of good report; if there

VII. Defeating The Spirit Of Depression, Fear, And Anxiety

be any praise, think on these things." We must protect our mind. Our mind is the target. If we refuse the devil from entering our mind, he can't defeat us.

It becomes a real effort when the negative thoughts in our minds have so deeply settled that they become a stronghold. When we entertain negative thoughts, many more wicked spirits come as a reinforcement to their attack. It is most important that we learn to capture the negative thoughts sent to us by the enemy. Second Corinthians 10:5 says, "Casting down imaginations, and every high thing that exalt itself against the knowledge of God, and bringing into *captivity* every thought to the obedience of Christ" (emphasis added). Those fiery darts must be intercepted and must be heavily resisted by the Word of God.

We do not have to give in to the destructive fear that the devil sends us. Satan has no legal right to bring fear into our life. We are to be very selective what we accept to believe. We are to listen only to words that agree with God's Word. On one side is Satan's destructive fear. On the other side is the powerful Spirit of power, of love, and of sound mind, which comes from the Almighty God (2 Tim. 1:7).

As we meditate (whisper/mutter) the Word of God slowly, we are planting the Word of God as precious seeds into our spirit. It needs to be deeply rooted and fully established to prevent the devil from uprooting it. Mark 4:15 states, "Satan cometh immediately and taketh away the Word that was sown in their hearts."

In Western movies, those cowboys who have learned the fast draw with their guns usually win. We have also seen how the Patriot missiles have successfully intercepted the Scud missiles that Saddam Hussein sent during the war in Iraq. As we learn to recognize that the devil is trying to send fiery darts into our minds, the sooner we can prevent our mind from receiving incoming negative thoughts. We must learn the "fast draw" to intercept incoming fiery darts with our sword, the Word of God. We need to learn how to counterattack (quick response) with the Word of God. This simple trick is very powerful and makes us strong overcomers. Keep visualizing the destruction it is causing the camp of the enemy when we keep releasing the Word through our meditation.

The Orthodox Jews know how to meditate, and we see them bobbing their heads as they keep whispering the Torah near the famous wailing walls in Jerusalem. Those Jews have practically memorized the entire Torah (the first five books of our Bible). Truly amazing! Other religions also recognize the power of meditation; but they use it for the wrong reason. Some Tibetan monks have been known to survive freezing temperatures with only flimsy clothing. However, we know that the power they possess comes from Satan, and they are being greatly deceived. Meditation has so much power, and it can be used for good or bad.

Many believers have suffered from depression and fear because they do not know how to resist the devil. Many continue to suffer severely for lack of knowledge. Hosea 4:6 says, "My people perish for lack of knowledge." If it is a severe depression, the fight against the devil will take time. The devil and his disciples will try to resist being dislodged from their victims. These wicked spirits got so used to being inside a person's mind that they think it is now their home.

Our salvation and deliverance from the spirits of fear and depression is in our total reliance and belief in the Word of God. It is hard to believe the Word of God when the devil blocks the Word of God from staying in our spirits. The only way to drive the devil away is through our persistent meditation. When we meditate on the Word of God, it will eventually start to take root in our spirit and will grow in us as we keep on with our meditation. Why allow the devil to win over our minds when we can soundly defeat him with our sword, the Word of God. The Word of God is our very potent weapon against the devil.

While we are sure of total victory, the battle of the mind is something that we need to work on. Our deliverance won't happen overnight. We need patience while learning how to meditate, but our deliverance and breakthrough will come. The Word of God guarantees it. The Word of God will never fail us. While waiting, the Lord will use this time to build our spiritual muscles.

VII. Defeating The Spirit Of Depression, Fear, And Anxiety

As we keep meditating on the Word of God consistently and often, the devil won't have any choice but to flee from us. When that happens, the depression that has haunted us for so long will be gone and we will be free from the spirit of depression. The devil and his demons will try to come back and to find out if we are maintaining our meditation. The key to fighting the devil is constant meditation.

We don't quit meditating until the devil has retreated. We must force the devil and his demons to withdraw and flee. It must be a forceful evacuation of the evil spirits from our mind. Our meditation must become a way of life to allow our spirit to grow strong each day. Our spirit must be loaded and fully armed with the Word of God.

When meditating on the Word of God, it is important to say it slowly and think carefully of the scripture verses we are meditating on. It is like chewing our food slowly, tasting every morsel we eat. It is also important to remember that the Word of God cannot really help us until it is deeply rooted in our spirit. When it is fully established and deeply rooted, the devil will no longer be able to uproot it.

The Word of God, when it is well entrenched in our spirits, becomes our powerful offensive weapon. To have an arsenal of weapons, we glue blank pages at the back of our Bible and keep writing down key Bible passages. We look at them often and select verses that we want to meditate on for each day. John 6:63, says, "The Word that I speak unto you is alive and has a spirit." We need to keep adding Bible verses to our list to expand our arsenal. More Bible passages are in the last section of this book to aid us. Hebrews 4:12 says, "For the Word of God is quick, and powerful, and sharper than any two edged sword, piercing even to the dividing asunder of soul and spirit." The Lord shows us how to use the Word of God to boldly confront the devil.

When we continue to meditate on the Word of God on a consistent basis, we will find that we start to believe the Word of God and our faith will exponentially grow. The Word of God will become alive in our spirits. Romans 10:17 tells us that our faith will grow by hearing—and hearing the Word of God. A lot of believers think that listening to sermons is what this verse is all about; but this is not what this verse is saying to us. It is listening to the pure Word of God through our meditation. If listening to the sermons is adequate to build faith, we should be seeing a formidable and victorious body of Christ. Instead, we see many weak and struggling believers among many congregations.

Listening to sermons is very good, and we highly recommend listening to anointed sermons. It helps us further understand the Word of God; but it is hearing and hearing or by whispering and whispering the Word of God that you need to do, in order to make our spirits hear it. Our spirits need to keep hearing the pure Word of God often to build strong faith. What we often plant into our spirits is what we will eventually become. Make a careful study of Psalms 1 and 119 and Joshua 1:8. These passages will give a better understanding of what meditation is all about.

Powerful meditation is the secret the devil is trying so hard to hide from us believers in order to capture the minds of many. The devil will try hard to uproot the Word of God from being planted in our spirits. Visualize the Word of God as our lethal weapon, cutting down the demons from entering our mind. There is no way that the devil can mount a successful attack against us when our spirit is heavily impregnated with the Word of God.

Second Timothy 1:7 says, "For God did not give us the spirit of fear, but of power, of love and of sound mind." This is a powerful sword against depression. This Bible verse tells us that fear has a spirit, and we must resist it by the sword of the Spirit, the Word of God. Our spirit need to hear this passage often through our meditation, whispering and whispering the Word, to build up our faith against spirits of fear and depression.

Powerful meditation means meditating on the Word of God while driving, washing, walking, and every opportunity we could find to whisper the Word of God. Meditation is transforming our mind to receive and agree with the Word of God. We become fully convinced of the Word of God when we keep meditating on it. Our meditation is now able to cancel out the lies of the devil; the wicked deception the devil sends doubts to discredit the Word of God.

VII. Defeating The Spirit Of Depression, Fear, And Anxiety

We are predisposed to believe bad news and entertain doubts in our mind since childhood. The devil has conditioned our mind to be negative. We shouldn't be surprised why it is so hard to fully believe the Word and God when we often entertain doubts. Romans 12:2 says, "And be not conformed to this world; but be ye transformed by the renewing of your mind, that ye may prove what is that good, acceptable, and perfect, will of God." Our meditation puts us in the fast lane where our faith can increase dramatically.

Ps. 138:2 says, "Thou has magnified Thy word above all thy name." God has lined up His whole reputation on His Word. He says that we should consider His Word be placed above His name. Why would God make this startling statement unless He is putting heavy emphasis on the integrity of His Word? God wants so much for us to believe His Word that He has declared such an awesome statement.

Here is the list of the author's preferred swords in resisting the devil:

1. Matthew 18:18—"... whatsoever ye shall bind on earth shall be bound in heaven; and whatsoever ye shall loose in earth shall be loosed in heaven."
2. Luke 10:19—"Behold, I give unto you power to tread on serpents and scorpions, and over all the power of the enemy; and nothing shall by any means hurt you."
3. Romans 8:37—"Nay, in all these things we are more than conquerors through Him that loved us."
4. 2 Corinthians 10:4—"For the weapons of our warfare are not carnal, but mighty through God to the pulling down of strongholds."
5. 1 John 4:4—"Ye are of God, little children, and have overcome them; because greater is He that is in you, than he that is in the world."
6. 2 Timothy 1:7—"For God didn't give us the spirit of fear, but of power, of love and of sound mind."
7. Isaiah 54:17—"No weapon that is formed against thee shall prosper ..."
8. Nehemiah 8:10—"... for the joy of the Lord is your strength."

9. 2 Corinthians 5:7—"We walk by faith; not by sight."
10. Acts 19:20—"So mightily grew in the word of God and prevailed."
11. 1 Thessalonians 5:18—"In everything give thanks; for this is the will of God in Christ Jesus concerning you."
12. Revelation 12:11—"And they overcame him by the blood of the Lamb and by the word of their testimony ..."

I personalized these passages, and I boldly say to the devil, "I take authority over you; I resist you and break your power. I bind you. I'm more than a conqueror, and I have been given authority over all the power of the enemy. Greater is He that is in me than he that is in the world. I pull down all your strongholds in Jesus' mighty name." I then keep whispering many passages until those spirits of fear and depression flee. They no longer come around as they used to, and when they do, they don't stay very long. They now know what to expect from me. I keep adding to my arsenal by reading, memorizing, and meditating on my list of passages written at the back of my Bible.

The devil will try hard to rob us of godly peace. The devil likes nothing more than for us to be agitated, confused, and fearful. Here are some Bible passages on peace:

1. Psalm 29:11—"The Lord will bless His people with peace ..."
2. Psalm 34:11—"... seek peace and pursue them."
3. Isaiah 26:3—"... perfect peace whose mind stays in Thee."
4. John 14:27—"Peace I leave with you, my peace I give unto you; not as the world giveth, give I unto you. Let not your heart be troubled, neither let it be afraid."
5. Colossians 3:15, "And let the peace of God rule in your hearts ..."

By simply meditating on those Bible passages, we will start to calm down and have godly peace. Meditating on those passages reminds us of the clear message of God's Word on peace. It allows our mind to focus on having peace, instead of being disturbed, dwelling on negative thoughts that the devil sends to upset us. Those passages are precious promises to us, and we need to receive them. If given a chance, and taken by faith, they will deliver and perform.

VII. Defeating The Spirit Of Depression, Fear, And Anxiety

At times when we have financial difficulties, we need to draw strength by meditating on God's Word. There are several Bible passages we could meditate on to give us faith on God to rescue us:

1. Matthew 6:33—"But seek ye first the kingdom of God, and his righteousness; and all these things shall be added unto you."
2. Philippians 4:19—"But my God shall supply all your need according to his riches in glory by Christ Jesus."
3. Psalm 73:26—"My flesh and my heart fail; but God is the strength of my heart, and my portion forever."
4. Psalm 31:24—"Be of good courage, and he shall strengthen your heart, all ye that hope in the Lord."

Meditating on the Word of God assures us of His promises. God is telling us to trust Him as our source. All the blessings and favor come from Him. He has unlimited resources to provide for us. He is the source of everything: love, strength, success, health, faith, prosperity, protection, and all we could think of. With His help, we will, not only be supplied with our needs, but we could give to those who are in need for God has inexhaustible source that cannot be depleted.

When we encounter spirits of fear and depression, we need to immediately dwell on the precious Word of God. When I first encountered those spirits of fear and depression, it took me several months resisting those malevolent spirits before they decided to flee. Nowadays, they do not stay very long, knowing I would continue with my meditation. Here are some Bible passages that will help us resist the spirit of fear:

1. Romans 8:15—"But ye have not received the spirit of bondage again to fear; but ye have received the Spirit of adoption, whereby we cry, Abba, Father."
2. Hebrews 13:6—"So that we may boldly say, the Lord is my helper, and I will not fear what man shall do unto me."
3. 2 Timothy 1:7—"For God hath not given us to the spirit of fear; but of power, of love, and of a sound mind."
4. Psalm 23:4—"... I will fear no evil."

At times, when spirits of doubts is attacking us, we must turn immediately to meditate on Bible passages that would nullify those malevolent spirits. Here are some powerful passages to mediate on:

1. Psalm 119:11—"Thy Word have I hid in mine heart, that I might not sin against Thee."
2. Psalm 119:105—"Thy Word is a lamp unto my feet, and a light unto my path."
3. Psalm 119:97," "O how I love thy Word! It is my meditation all the day."
4. Proverbs 3:5—"Trust in the Lord with all thine heart and lean not on thine own understanding. In all thy ways acknowledge him and he shall direct thy paths."
5. 1 Peter 2:9—"But ye are a chosen generation, a royal priesthood, a holy nation, a peculiar people; that ye should show forth they praises of him who hath called you out of darkness into His marvelous light."

The steps to follow on meditation is simply choosing the right Bible passages to meditate on (whispering/muttering) to aid us against our problems. It is like having the right keys to unlock our doors. Our spirit need to hear the Word of God often to gain strong faith. We need to meditate during most of our free time. Many believers do not realize the awesome power of the Word of God to help them.

The key to winning against the spirits of fear and depression is forcing our mind to continually think of the Word and not submit to the fearful thoughts that the devil continuously tries to send. We just need to keep refusing to receive the wicked lies of the devil. He is a master liar, and he doesn't play fair. We need to train our spirit through our meditation to listen to the Word carefully. We need to focus on the Bible passages we are meditating on in order to deny the devil any entry to our mind. This practice takes time, but we need to stay with it. There is no way the devil can win if we learn to stay focused on the Word of God. We just need to keep dwelling on it so that it totally occupies our mind. Not dwelling on thoughts or actions that could trigger depression will also serve us well.

VII. Defeating The Spirit Of Depression, Fear, And Anxiety

One very important rule to remember in fighting the spirit of fear and depression is to not ever give up. Never give up. If we do, we are sending a strong signal to the devil that all he has to do is increase the pressure of his attack, and we will give up. It will help us to remember the powerful instruction for us in 2 Corinthians 10:5, that says, "Casting down imaginations, and every high thing that exalt itself against the knowledge of God, and bringing into captivity every thought to the obedience of Christ." We are bringing into captivity all the fiery darts that the devil is forcing into our minds by our continuously resisting it with our meditation. We keep intercepting all the fiery darts of the devil to deny it any entry. Trust the Word of God to fight for us.

Because the devil is relentless, blocking the incoming fiery darts is not easy to do, but this is how we can train our minds to resist the negative thoughts the devil keeps sending to us. We must deny the devil any entry into our minds by focusing and dwelling intensely on the Word of God. If we sense that the fight is becoming more difficult and fiercer, it could only mean that the devil is unleashing all his might to defeat us, but this is also signaling that his stronghold is diminishing and his defeat is near. After he has thrown his knockout punch, and we are still standing and resisting, he has no other option but to retreat and flee. Our dedication to stay with the Word of God sets us free from fear and depression.

We need to keep asserting our authority over the devil by learning to appropriate the effective and awesome power of the Word of God. Military parlance says, "The best defense is offense." Our continuous offensive and counterattack will put the devil and his cohorts at bay. We visualize slashing with our lethal weapon that is a sharp two-edged sword. It is cutting down the enemies as they come. We must remind ourselves over and over again the need to press a strong counterattack whenever the devil starts an attack. We need to show no fear. The devil is reading our reaction on his attacks. Satan must be convinced that his attacks are not working and ineffective against us. Nothing would please the devil more than seeing us cowering in fear whenever he launches an attack.

Again, the battleground is our mind. It is the primary target of the enemy. The devil is always probing for our weak spots. His attacks will be in the area of our weaknesses. If the devil thinks he can win, he will be relentless in his attacks. However, as skillful as our adversary is, his attacks will be futile and nullified when we keep intercepting his fiery darts with our precision weapon, the Word of God. We will lose only if we don't put up a fight and treat the Word of God carelessly as if it has no power to resist the devil. However, barring such thought, the joy of living can be achieved by defeating the spirit of fear, anxiety, and depression. There are just so many ways that the Word of God can help us.

Fear comes in many forms. If we have experienced being ridiculed, made to look like a fool, made fun of, being rejected or made to feel not accepted in some circles, these incidents were carefully designed by the devil to try to minimize our self-worth. We must resist this negative experience embedded in our minds and not accept it as our true self. The devil often uses insensitive, evil, and crude people to malign us. These type of people take pleasure in seeing the suffering of others. The more we become susceptible, the more the devil will continue harassing us. Millions have become victims of the devil, not knowing that they can resist the devil through the Word of God. All these efforts from the devil are to make us feel worthless, to have many doubts, and to dislike ourselves. The devil does not want us to see how God sees us—we are complete in Christ.

When this sinking feeling of returning to a hurtful past comes, we must resist it at once by our sword, the Word of God. The devil keeps attacking us from several directions to try to weaken us greatly. The devil wants to keep us off balance by sending fear and condemnation. The devil takes pleasure in reminding us of our many mistakes. He wants to keep us from our comfort zone. The devil will continue his barrage of negative thoughts until we learn to stop him. Romans 8:2 says, "There is no now no condemnation to them which are in Christ Jesus, who walk no after the flesh, but after the spirit." This is a great Bible passage against the spirit of condemnation. This spirit of condemnation is a strong weapon that the devil uses often to try to upset us. We just to keep remembering that the devil is a liar, and what he is throwing at us are all lies.

When we are fully engaged in meditation on a consistent basis, the devil can no longer lie to us, telling us that the Word of God doesn't work and unreliable. Our faith in the Word of God, through our meditation, nullifies and renders the attacks of the devil useless. While we used to tremble with depression and fear, our meditation has now put us in the driver's seat. The devil can no longer toy with our minds. We have clearly won. The only way we can lose is if we neglect our prayer, study, and meditation of the Word.

We need to resist any attack from the devil and fight for our minds. Whenever we are attacked, we launch an immediate and full retaliatory counterattack against the forces of Satan. Being angry, restless, and confused are some of the devil's favorite weapons. Be fully aware that it is the devil who is giving us those destructive thoughts and feelings. Any negative thoughts that you are receiving are coming from the devil and we must be resist them at once by the Word of God. The devil heavily employs sneak attacks, and he would inject doubts into our minds when we least expect it to further undermine our faith.

Most of the efforts of the devil is to try to capture our mind. It is the battlefield. Mayo clinic (Depression—Mayo Clinic 1998–2015. Mayo Foundation for Medical Education and Research) describes depression as a disease of the mind. Medical clinics cannot adequately explain why their patients with depression keep receiving wicked thoughts. Where did those wicked thoughts come from, and why do they keep coming? The medical community fails to give an accurate answer. Millions who are suffering from deep depression have encountered similar symptoms of unexplained feeling of hopelessness, panic, and trauma. However, we believers know the answer to it because it says in 2 Timothy 1:7 that it is the spirit of fear that is causing it. Spiritual battles must be fought heavily in the spirit realm to defeat those wicked spirits of fear and depression.

At times, the devil would launch a fierce and massive attack on our mind without any warning. He would try to ram his wicked thoughts to our minds repeatedly to try to break our defenses. When this happens, it is a signal for us to start praising the Lord and start meditating on the Word. The devil hates it when we start praising the Lord and start releasing the Word. We must stay focused on the meditation of the Word. Our minds can only think one thought at a time; either we are entertaining wicked thoughts coming from the devil, or we are dwelling on the Word of God. Fierce attacks from the devil must be met with our superior firepower and heavily armed weaponry, the Word of God. The devil and his cohorts will get the idea that we are committed to fight, and they will have to flee.

We will do well in life if we heed the vital instructions of the Lord to meditate on His Word often (day and night). It is estimated that there are hundreds of millions suffering from depression around the world. Meditation is the key to overcoming the spirits of depression and fear. Meditation must be a way of life. This is the deciding factor on who wins or loses in the fight of our mind.

BONUS SECTION
VIII. THE VITAL MINISTRY OF THE HOLY SPIRIT

The Holy Spirit is the third person in the Trinity. He is fully God. He is eternal, omniscient, and omnipresent. He has a will and can speak. He is alive. He is a person, contrary to the teachings of the cults that He is a force and not a being. He has a tremendous ministry in helping believers. However, He is not very visible in the Bible because His ministry is to bear witness of Jesus Christ.

The devil will try very hard to prevent us from having a close fellowship with the Holy Spirit. We supercharge our relationship with our heavenly Father and with our Lord Jesus Christ with the help of the Holy Spirit. In life, we are faced with so many decisions to make, and we often do not know which decision is the right one to make. Why not ask the Holy Spirit for help, as He is more than willing to assist us in life?

We can do nothing by ourselves, but He that is in us, the Holy Spirit, will win the victory. Recognize that it's not us who has to deal with the devil but the Holy Spirit that is in us. Communing with the Holy Spirit makes us like an eagle flying in the sky, soaring in the wind currents and flying effortlessly. Acts 1:8 says, "But ye shall receive power, after that the Holy Ghost is come upon you ..."

Understand that we won't be able to win over the devil on our own strength, but the Holy Spirit residing in us gets it done.

Having the patience to learn the ministry of the Holy Spirit will pay a rewarding dividend. Believers hardly consult the Holy Spirit and the devil often beats them badly for their spiritual ignorance. Hosea 4:6 says, "My people perish for lack of knowledge."

The Holy Spirit indwells every believer who have received and committed to Christ Jesus. The Holy Spirit who dwells in us brings power into our life. This is the only way a believer can fulfill his ministry, and it is done through the power of the Holy Spirit.

Some of the Awesome Ministries of the Holy Spirit

1. *The Holy Spirit testifies that we are God's children.* Romans 8:15–16 says, "For ye have not received the spirit of bondage again to fear; but ye have received the Spirit of adoption, whereby we cry, Abba, Father. The Spirit itself bear witness with our spirit, that we are the children of God."
2. *The Holy Spirit intercedes in our behalf.* Romans 8:26–27 says, "Likewise the Spirit also help our infirmities. For we know not what we should pray for as we ought; but the Spirit itself make intercession for us with such groaning which cannot be uttered. And he that search the hearts know what is the mind of the Spirit, because He make intercession for the saints according to the will of God."
3. *The Holy Spirit gives us joy and peace.* Galatians 5:22–23 says, "But the fruit of the Spirit is love, joy, peace, longsuffering, gentleness, goodness, faith, meekness, temperance, against such there is no law."
4. *The Holy Spirit gives us the gift of ministry.* Second Corinthians 4:1 says, "Therefore, seeing we have this ministry, as we have received mercy, we faint not."
5. *The Holy Spirit gives us boldness to witness.* First Timothy 3:13 says, "For they that have used the office of a deacon will purchase to themselves a good degree, and great boldness in the faith which is in Christ Jesus."
6. *The Holy Spirit helps us pray.* Ephesians 6:18 says, "Praying always with all prayer and supplications in the Spirit, and

watching thereunto with all perseverance and supplication for all saints."
7. *The Holy Spirit gives us the spirit of wisdom and revelation.* Ephesians 1:17, 18 says, "That the God of our Lord Jesus Christ, the Father of glory, may give unto you the spirit of wisdom and revelation in the knowledge of him. The eyes of your understanding being enlightened; that ye may know what is the hope of his calling, and what the riches of the glory of his inheritance in the saints."
8. *God speaks through us by the Holy Spirit.* Matthew 10:20 says, "For it is not ye that speak but the Spirit of your Father which speak to you."
9. *The Holy Spirit is our teacher, guiding us to all truth.* John 16:13 says, "Howbeit when He, the Spirit of truth is come, He will guide you into all truth; for he shall not speak of himself; but whatsoever he shall hear, that shall he speak, and he will show you things to come."
10. *The Holy Spirit purifies believers.* Romans 8:1–2 says, "I beseech you therefore, brethren, by the mercies of God, that ye present your bodies a living sacrifice, holy, acceptable unto God, which is your reasonable service. And be not conformed to this world; but be ye transformed by the renewing of your mind, that ye may prove what is that good, and acceptable, and perfect, will of God."
11. *The Holy Spirit gives us power.* Zechariah 4:6 says, "Not by might, nor by power, but by my spirit, said the Lord of hosts."

Symbols of the Holy Spirit

1. *Dove.* Matthew 3:16 says, "… he saw the Spirit of God, descending like a dove and lighting upon him."
2. *Wind.* Acts 2:2 says, "And suddenly there came a sound from heaven as of a rushing mighty wind, and it filled all the house where they were sitting."
3. *Fire.* Acts 2:3 says, "And there appeared unto them cloven tongues like as of fire, and it sat upon each of them."

Sins we commit against the Holy Spirit

1. *By blasphemy.* Matthew 12:24 says, "But when the Pharisees heard it, they said, this fellow doth not cast out devils, but by Beelzebub, the prince of the devils."
2. *By resisting.* Acts 7:51 says, "Ye stiff necked and uncircumcised in heart and ears, ye do always resist the Holy Spirit, as your fathers did, so do ye."
3. *By insults.* Hebrews 10:29 says, "Of how much sorer punishment, suppose ye, shall he be thought worthy, who hath trodden down under foot the Son of God, and hath counted the blood of the covenant, wherewith he was sanctified, an unholy thing, and hath done despite unto the Spirit of grace?"
4. *By lying.* Acts 5:3 says, "But Peter said, Ananias, why hath Satan filled thine heart to lie to the Holy Spirit and to keep back part of the price of the land?"
5. *By grieving.* Ephesians 4:30 says, "And grieve not the holy Spirit of God, whereby ye are sealed unto the day of redemption."
6. *By quenching.* First Thessalonians 5:19 says, "Quench not the Spirit."

The Fruit of the Holy Spirit (Galatians 5:22–23)

1. Love
2. Joy
3. Peace
4. Longsuffering
5. Gentleness
6. Goodness
7. Faith
8. Meekness
9. Temperance

Diversities of Gifts of the Holy Spirit (1 Corinthians 12:4–10)

1. The word of knowledge
2. The word of wisdom

3. The gift of prophecy
4. The gift of faith
5. The gift of healing
6. The working of miracles
7. The discerning of spirits
8. The different kind of tongues
9. The interpretation of tongues

The Holy Spirit has a vital role in helping us in our earthly journey. We cannot do many things in life without the vital help of the Holy Spirit. Being the executive of the Trinity, He helps us in so many ways to make us succeed in our Christian walk. The ministry of the Holy Spirit is so awesome, and we just need to experience it.

When Jesus left for heaven, He promised to leave us the Comforter, the Holy Spirit. This is an awesome help coming from the Lord; sending the Holy Spirit to guide us. The Holy Spirit, the executive of the Trinity, was sent to us and yet not too many believers grasp the full measure of the help the Holy Spirit is willing to give them. The Bible says we have not because we ask not. How often do we ask the Holy Spirit for help? Why not ask the Holy Spirit, who is omniscient and has the power to help us, for the help we need? We forfeit so much available help and blessings from the Holy Spirit by neglecting to ask Him.

The only way we can walk with the Holy Spirit is to make a direct contact with Him, to start a vital relationship with him. We need to open up to Him, sharing our life with Him, and inviting Him to fellowship with us. The Holy Spirit will come with our heartfelt invitation. The Holy Spirit will then begin to work with us in many areas of our lives to become what God has intended us to be. Begin by asking the Holy Spirit to help us in difficult areas in our life. Nothing is too big or too small for the Holy Spirit. He is more than willing to assist us in our difficulties. He will give us wisdom and help us with our problems in our work, our family, friends, and all things that are important to us. The Holy Spirit is just waiting to be asked, and He will be happy to counsel us. Not understanding the vital ministry of the Holy Spirit has affected the spiritual strength of many believers.

I have had many experiences receiving help from the Holy Spirit. There were several occasions when I got lost driving on the busy freeway. I got distracted, thinking of certain chores I need to do, and I would completely miss my exit. I was having a hard time finding my way, and I was completely lost. The moment I asked the Holy Spirit to show me the way out, it was not long that I would find my way back. The ministry of the Holy Spirit to help us is truly amazing.

One experience that I could never forget was the time we were financially hard up. It was so bad that we didn't even know where to find money for the next day. This went on for a couple years; our faith was being severely tested. Up to now, it is so hard for me to explain how we managed to survive those very lean years. Only the Holy Spirit could rescue and help us when the situation looked so helpless. That experience has fortified our faith in God, knowing He will always be there for us. Our God is truly a faithful God. Testing and trials allow our faith to grow.

I cannot forget the times when the Holy Spirit helped me make the right decisions. In several important occasions, I needed to make the right decision, and I was clueless which decision to make. The moment I asked the Holy Spirit to guide me to make the right decision, without fail, He impressed upon me the right decision to make. I peppered my request with much prayer and meditation, and the Holy Spirit guided me in the decision to make.

The Holy Spirit should be our best friend in this planet. God the Father sits on His throne in heaven. God the Son, our Lord Jesus Christ, sits at right hand of the Father in heaven. The Holy Spirit is left on earth to help us directly. He was sent here to encourage us to be faithful and continuously remind us of God's awesome love. He is a very important and powerful person in our lives. We will never be able to relate to God correctly until we understand the awesome ministry of the Holy Spirit. If we want power in our lives, we need the help of the Holy Spirit. He is the one directly involved with us in our day-to-day lives. Opening up to the Holy Spirit does not mean we are minimizing our love for God and our Lord Jesus Christ. The Holy Spirit helps us even in our prayers to God.

VIII. The Vital Ministry Of The Holy Spirit

The world is so fortunate that the Holy Spirit is here on earth, preventing the devil from unleashing his unrestrained wrath. The Holy Spirit is the restraining power keeping the devil in check. The moment the Holy Spirit is taken away from the Earth, chaos, nuclear war, and devastation will most likely hit the whole earth. It is most probable that the huge stockpile of nuclear bombs possessed by many countries will explode, killing billions of people. The massive nuclear explosion will create a massive opening in the ozone layers in the heavens, allowing the sun to send its blazing and searing heat into earth. The earth will be so warm that it would melt the ice in the North and South poles, causing tidal waves and massive flooding in many coastal cities. Many regions will turn into a total wasteland. The heat will kill many fishes in the ocean and destroy many trees and plants. Forest fires will be rampant. Many small islands in the Pacific Ocean will most likely disappear. It will be the worst catastrophic event the world has ever known.

Those who start fellowshipping with the Holy Spirit in an intimate way will have a life-changing experience. Without a doubt, the discovery of the power of the Holy Spirit to assist us in life is extraordinary. Believers, who have experienced a close fellowship with the Holy Spirit, cannot have a mediocre Christian life. Something super and wonderful await those who learn to have a genuine loving fellowship with the Holy Spirit. Faithful believers who engage the Holy Spirit in their lives will truly experience a great spiritual journey. It is a most rewarding and awesome Christian life.

We need to learn how to consult the Holy Spirit often. We will find our lives so much easier to handle with His help. This is something we need to practice and learn daily. Most believers are not acquainted with the important ministry of the Holy Spirit, and they go through life aimlessly without His help. The Holy Spirit is more than willing to help us, if we start involving Him in our day-to-day lives. We will be very blessed with His help. Many times, we believers have received help without realizing it came from the Holy Spirit.

There was a time in Heidi Baker's ministry in the tiny nation of Mozambique in Africa when she experienced help from the Holy Spirit. The Muslim authorities in their region hated Christians and ordered them to leave their orphanage compound immediately. They had no choice but to leave, or they would all be put in prison. Over 200 young orphan children had to travel several miles to the nearest station. The children were tired and hungry when they arrived, but there was no food. A consulate officer heard of their plight, and she brought some food for Heidi, not knowing there are over 200 children to be fed. Heidi asked the children to bow and pray for their dinner, and the food that was just enough to feed one family kept multiplying for over 200 children. All the children were fed.

Many times, the Holy Spirit comes to our aid in desperate times. One incident happened in Kenya during the dreaded Mau Mau rebellion in the 1950s. Those rebels were killing foreigners and missionaries who crossed their path. One group of missionaries was very close to the rebels and needed to leave at once. It so happened that the gas fuel line of their bus broke. This group prayed for guidance from the Holy Spirit since they had no spare part to replace the broken fuel line. He impressed upon them to bore a hole into a raw potato to connect the broken fuel lines, and they were able to restart their vehicle just in the nick of time. The Mau Mau rebels were almost upon them.

Our son Peter has a remarkable experience with the Holy Spirit. He and his friend Aaron were painting a dorm house near their Bible college in Twin Peaks, a town in San Bernardino, California. They had finished painting for the day, and Aaron was looking for his car keys that he has misplaced. They looked in every nook and corner of the house but could not find his keys. They decided to pray where to look, and the Holy Spirit impressed upon them to look in the paint bucket. Sure enough, the keys had fallen in the paint bucket. Normally, that would be the last place to look. What are the odds of the car keys falling inside the paint bucket? The ministry of the Holy Spirit is truly so awesome. We forfeit our many blessings and opportunities in life by not asking the help of the Holy Spirit.

IX. THE CHALLENGE TO STUDY AND MEDITATE

The Holy Scripture is our precious gift from God. We must learn to value it. We need to study the Bible, starting with the New Testament, one chapter after the other, in consecutive order and book by book. It is important that we read our Bible in consecutive order. This will assist us in clearly understanding the holy Word of God. Persistency and perseverance are required to develop strong faith. Even in studying in school, we are required to keep reading and reviewing books assigned to us to better prepare us for the coming exams. It takes time for our mind to absorb information, and so we continue to try to remember by reading and memorizing what we need to learn.

Physical therapists strongly instruct their clients to do daily exercises repeatedly to develop a habit. They undergo rigid training and exercise to produce the intended results. Habit in physical exercise or spiritual study and meditation do not come easy for us. It is necessary to reinforce our daily routine to have a strong effect on us. Some of the instructions in this book have been repeated again and again to reinforce and remind the readers the need to follow vital instructions as suggested in this book.

Continuous repetition is what will help us to excel in our goal. A person can hardly excel in his or her chosen field of endeavor without committing to a daily effort of attaining his or her goal.

Doing the repetitions is often called mastery. We can ask ourselves, why does the world put all kinds of sacrifices and effort to worldly pursuits, when the only real meaningful pursuit in life worth doing is understanding and planting the Word of God into our spirits?

The challenge is to commit into a godly pursuit that would significantly help us in our lives' journey and prepare us for eternal life in heaven. Our mindset is to aim on what is eternal and to not give way to any temporal ambition. Will it be easy to commit to a lifelong commitment on our study and meditation? The answer will depend on our priorities in life. The study of the Bible and meditation of the Word will take time, and it will take real commitment and self-discipline.

Here are some of the hindrances and enemies of meditation

1. The devil stealing the Word of God
2. Being too preoccupied with life
3. Being too impatient to see if the Word of God works
4. Having no real commitment to serve God
5. It is not a priority in life to learn the Bible
6. Not seeing any real value in studying and meditating on the Word of God
7. Having a negative and doubtful mind
8. Being with friends who have no spiritual interest at all

Life is an arduous journey. It is full of pitfalls, challenges, and uncertainties. It is like traveling at night in a deep, dense forest, not seeing where we are going. In the midst of such darkness, the good Lord offers His precious Word to guide us. Psalm 119:105 says, "Thy Word is a lamp unto my feet, and a light unto my path." We are safe to travel with the Word of God serving as our light. It is, however, becoming a perilous journey without any light from the Word of God to shine our path. It becomes extremely dangerous to travel in life without the divine guidance of the Word of God. The many important decisions we make in life affect us greatly in life. Why not allow the Word of God to give us wisdom to make the right decisions?

IX. The Challenge To Study And Meditate

A good case in point was when I was preparing to write this book. I was experiencing much uncertainty and trepidation while thinking of writing a book. I knew I had to somehow share my experience in learning to resist spirits of fear and depression, but writing a book was the farthest thing from my mind. I have to ask the Holy Spirit to let me know if I should even consider writing a book. After receiving encouragement and peace from God, peppered with His Word, this book started to take its form. Without the help of the Holy Spirit and the meditation of the Word of God, this book would have not been written.

If we observe carefully, we will find ourselves often thinking negatively without being aware of it. We often see the negative sides of life, like doubting Thomas, hard to convince with new ideas and things. We often find yourselves viewing things negatively. We see the "what if" negative side of things. Many great accomplishments could have been made if only people with ideas learned to proceed with some faith. We have heard of gold prospectors stopping just a few feet away of hitting the motherlode of gold, that would have given them enormous riches. We sense a deep loss for those gold prospectors, but we are also guilty of giving up on some of our good ideas.

It would be an exercise in futility if we based our hope on the Word of God if it's not true. If not true, God makes Himself a liar, and the truth is not in Him. However, we believers know that God cannot lie, and the truth *is* in Him. The God that we serve made a solemn promise of the integrity of His Word. Matthew 24:35 says, "Heaven and earth shall pass away, but my words shall not pass away." The Holy Spirit confirms this in our spirits to be true.

However, it would be a mistake to expect a dramatic change in our faith, after studying and meditating in the Word of God for only a few weeks. Do plants grow as trees in just a few weeks? The study and meditation of the Word of God takes time, but it produces enormous spiritual dividend. It is one of the best spiritual exercises we can do in life. We need to start a love affair with our Bible.

Why is it so necessary to do a daily study and meditation on the Word of God? When we look at a master artist like Rembrandt, do we see him painting his priceless artwork and then completely forgetting and abandoning it? A great artist spends many hours each day to develop what he has created, carefully putting in the right shades, lines, and color. Careful caring and nurturing of what we do are necessary to produce good results.

Our minds tend to gravitate to doubts and unbelief. The world has contaminated and conditioned our minds to be skeptical, and we have the need to first see before we can believe. Don't we ask ourselves why and what whenever people tell us something. We often scrutinize what people tell us and keep proving before we can accept what others say. People often exaggerate their stories, and we have learned to guard ourselves against what people tell us before believing and accepting them.

If we are not making good progress in our meditation, it is because the devil sends spirits of condemnation, which must be repelled. These spirits of condemnation are relentless and keep sending many accusations against us. Mistakes we have made many years ago suddenly keep coming back into our mind. We need to meditate on this passage to drive them away: Romans 8:1 says, "There is therefore now no condemnation to them which are in Christ Jesus, who walk not after the flesh, but after the spirit." We keep up with our meditation until we sense faith growing in our spirit. We do not allow the devil to sidetrack us.

The devil would like nothing better but to blur our mind so that we cannot understand the Word of God. The devil will put all kinds of thoughts and hindrances to capture our mind from understanding the Bible. We often hear people say that they cannot understand the Bible. The devil has succeeded in blinding their understanding. The Bible is meant for believers, and unbelievers simply would not be able to understand the holy teachings of Christ. Romans 8:9 says, "Now if any man has not the Spirit of Christ, he is none of His." The Word of God is spiritually discerned, and only believers who study the Bible can understand it.

The Word of God is our guide. Without the Word of God, we would live in total darkness. Nothing is more alarming than traveling in an isolated road, not knowing where to go. In the olden days, travelers traveled in the daytime and pitched their tents at night. Likewise, we would be lost when we journey through life without the guidance of the holy Word of God. The world is full of uncertainties and great peril without the beacon light of the Word of God to shine on our path.

The encompassing Word of God has guided and delivered a multitude of believers through the ages. It will protect us against the wiles and cunning of the devil. We read in the Bible that Jesus Himself used the Word of God against the devil when He was severely tempted in the wilderness. If the devil has the audacity to attack the Lord, he won't hesitate in attacking us. The devil was no match against the Word of God, and when the Lord uttered the Word, the devil was forced to flee. When responding to the attacks of the devil, we need to be careful and deliberate in whispering the Word. We must slow down and avoid hurrying in whispering the Word. Doing this would help us think on the Word we are planting into our spirit. The Lord Jesus shared with us His awesome experienced in dealing with the devil to show us how to resist the devil through the Word of God.

One of our authorities as the children of God is being able to resist and defeat the devil. Luke 10:19 says, "Behold, I give unto you power to tread on serpents and scorpions, and over all the power of the enemy; and nothing shall by any means hurt you." We need to meditate on this passage to believe our full and awesome authority over the devil. This passage has to have deep roots in our spirit through our meditation, so we do not waver in our belief. This passage clearly declares our clear authority over the devil. It is a delegated authority. Our Lord Jesus Christ has soundly defeated the devil, and He has transferred this power to us. Many times, our meditation does not make sense to us, but we keep at it. This is like traveling on a deserted highway, and all we see are more roads until we finally arrive at our destination.

If we truly believe this delegated authority given to us by the Lord Jesus Christ, then we should be bold in facing the devil when he comes around. The Lord says we can defeat the devil, and if we believe this to be true, then the devil has to flee. We can only be defeated if we refuse to believe the Word of God or if we lack the knowledge of our authority. The devil will sense if we truly believe the Word of God, and he will continue to launch a series of attacks to see how we will react. We either give up or keep fighting, using the Word.

This is where meditation will greatly help to fortify our faith in believing the Word of God. Romans 8:28 says, "And we know that all things work together for good to them that love God and are called according to His purpose." If we say we believe the Word of God, then we can rest on His promises. God Himself guarantees the power of His Word. The Word of God works if we believe in it without doubting and wavering. My wife has shared with me on several occasions that meditating on the Word of God has truly changed her life. Several things that used to bother her have no longer affected her after learning to meditate on the Word of God. The meditation of the Word has truly given her the joy of living.

My good friend Lydia has developed a habit of sharing Bible passages to others almost on a daily basis on Facebook. This wonderful habit has given her enormous joy and spiritual richness through her daily meditation of the Word. I cannot help but notice the big change in her countenance. She has so much peace of God.

My close friend Burt eagerly testified to me that learning to meditate on the Word of God has made him more courageous and not fearful as he used to be. Before learning to meditate on the Word, he was so afraid to ride an elevator by himself. The spirit of fear had caused him to be afraid of being alone inside an elevator. He overcame a stronghold of fear with the Word of God. He has become a courageous overcomer.

I had another wonderful experience with a friend who has greatly benefited from godly meditation. My good friend Alelee has learned to meditate and has appreciated the great value of it. We moved to another city and missed contacts, and I didn't see her until several years later. When I saw her again, she was so excited in sharing with me how the meditation she has learned had helped her with the serious illness of her brother. She shared with her brother the power of the Word of God. Fortunately, he believed her and fully embraced what Alelee had shared with him. He meditated continuously on

IX. The Challenge To Study And Meditate

Bible passages on healing and, by God's grace, he was completely cured of cancer. The Word of God is truly full of power when we embrace and totally believe it.

The Bible was written for our great benefit. We must heed the instructions in the Bible to protect us against the continuous assaults of the devil to undermine us. The devil has no mercy and takes great pleasure in inflicting great pain and suffering to mankind. However, you can take comfort that John 10:10b says, "I am come that they may have life and have it more abundantly." This tells us that our Lord has defeated the devil soundly, and the devil no longer has any power over us.

We need to pay clear and undivided attention when reading and learning the instructions coming from the Bible. We must learn to navigate and use it well in time of need. Very fortunate are those who have diligently read the Bible and carefully followed its instructions. Knowledge is power, and the knowledge written in the Bible gives us a decisive advantage against the devil.

I would have been not motivated to write this book without first experiencing the awesome power of the Word of God to help me. The unspeakable agony and suffering I have experienced from a very severe depression led me to study and research the Bible on how to defeat the devil with the Word of God. In a nutshell, it was prayer, study, and meditation of the Word of God that has set me free from the bondage of fear and depression.

I now know that it was my calling to write this book to help many others to total freedom from the ailments and sufferings they face. The study of the Word of God is to not only combat fear and depression but also the many problems we face in life. The solution is to find appropriate Bible passages to address our problems, meditating on them and staying on them until great victory have been won. The Bible is fully equipped to help us in all areas of difficulties when we submit to the study and meditation of the Word of God. Trust the Word of God completely, and it will not disappoint us. However, strong faith comes only when we fully commit to the study and meditation of the Word of God.

Life is a journey. There are hazardous journeys and pleasant journeys. A difficult journey could be filled with many mishaps and unforeseen danger due to lack of preparation. Wise travelers know how to prepare properly for their long journey. They prepare themselves in case of some unforeseen events. Nothing could be more frustrating to travelers than to be stranded in some deserted area. We all know the danger of being ill prepared, and yet how many people travel recklessly without the necessary preparation.

Traveling should be an enjoyable experience. We get to see many new beautiful places while driving along scenic routes. Traveling is a lot of fun, and many have enjoyed fun memories in their travels. Many families spend quality vacation each year. It is one of the fun things to do in life. However, it is prudent to be well prepared before embarking on any travel. We must not be overlook preparation.

A more important journey is the spiritual journey in life, which requires a more serious preparation. Without the daily study and meditation of the Word of God, strong faith cannot be developed and sustained. The Bible is our manual for living. The Bible says whatever we sow, so shall we reap. Those Bible passages that we keep planting into our spirits through daily meditation will surely bring a good and bountiful harvest in due season. Galatians 6:7 says, "Be not deceived, God is not mocked, for whatsoever a man sow, that shall he also reap."

The study and meditation of the Word of God must be very important to our Lord, or He wouldn't bother reminding us again and again to do it. As we diligently study and meditate on the Word of God, we will invariably notice the spiritual growth in our spirits. We will see real spiritual progress that we didn't think possible. Our spirits cannot help but grow with the consistent study and meditation of the holy Word of God.

In these last days, we must exhibit boldness in following and preaching the Word of God. Half of the battle has already been won through our diligent preparation. God wants us to have an activity of faith that dares to believe God. There is what seems like faith, an appearance of faith, but real faith believes God right to the end.

IX. The Challenge To Study And Meditate

We must allow our Lord Jesus Christ living inside us to control our lives. When we believe the Word of God, the virtue of Christ comes. Recognize that it is not we that will defeat the devil, but the greater One that is in us. It is the most wonderful life possible, a life of faith in the Son of God. Oh, for the simple faith to receive what God so lavishly offers. We can never be ordinary from the day we receive the life from above. We become extraordinary, filled with the extraordinary power of the extraordinary God. When we do what God says in His Word, our lives will be bright and right.

The more we know we are nothing, the more God can channel His power to us. If we rise up in love because we want to honor God, we will find the presence of God upon us. We ought to see that in the name of Jesus, there is power that is more than a match against all the forces of the enemies. Faith has a deaf ear to the devil and to the natural mind but big ears to God.

It is an important reminder for us to that we release spiritual power by constantly opening our mouth and boldly speaking God's Word. We will only experience the peace of God if we are able to turn away from our intellect and emotion, instead trusting God with a simple childlike faith.

We will not fear old age if spiritual renewal is constantly going on inside us. We refuse to react to fear, doubt and unbelief; instead, we let the awesome Word of God filter our reaction. It is learning to live without fear.

Principles to follow

1. Learn to relax and wait on God.
2. Do not press or try to force the issue.
3. The timing of our God is perfect.
4. We need to know that our God knows best.
5. We need to remain calm.
6. We must trust God completely.
7. Learn to ask the Holy Spirit to help us.

The Word of God becomes a mighty weapon when we release it. There are no "ifs" or "buts"; His promises are "yea" and "amen." All things are possible to them who believe. If the Word of God is fully established in our spirit, we will automatically react to what the Word of God say; instead of reacting with fear to the crisis we are faced with. Peace is oneness with God. God's Word is the storehouse; all of His power is stored in it. Its power is greater than anything that will ever come against us. If we want to be in the rising tide, we must accept all God has said in His Word. The Word of God tells us that God the Father loves us just as much as He loves His Beloved Son. God loves us that much. God's love is unconditional.

Pride and unbelief stop us from entering into God's rest, which can only be entered through humility and trust. Love is the key to the Kingdom of God. God Himself lives inside us. How awesome is that? We need to ponder the awesome and unspeakable love God has for us. Apostle Paul tells us that he manifestly declared himself to be the epistle of Christ, written not with ink, but with the Spirit of the Living God. We can declare the existence of God from everlasting to everlasting.

When we control our lives, we are like being in a prison. When the Holy Spirit controls our lives, we are free. We would be like the migratory birds that travel the vast ocean and are able to get into the wind current and glide, soaring high above the earth, letting the power of the strong wind to carry them.

When we spend quiet time with the Lord each day, we are actually setting up like an Earth satellite transmitting station that is a direct communication between the spiritual realm and the natural realm.

X. BECOMING AN OVERCOMER

Love is a force. The Bible says in 1 John 4:18, "perfect love casts out fear." If we know for certain that God loves us, what is there to fear? Isaiah 43:1 says, "Fear not, for I have redeemed thee, I have called thee by thy name; thou art mine." Jeremiah 29:11 says, "For I know the plans I have for you declares the lord. Plans to bless you and not to harm you. plans to give you hope and a future." We must learn to meditate on these kinds of passages and hold on to it. These are awesome promises of the Lord for us. We need to keep adding Bible passages at the back of our Bible for easy access and to aid us in our daily meditation.

We will be amazed at how much Bible verses we can retain by reading the list of selected Bible verses we have written at the back of our Bible often. Why is this practice so important? We read in the Bible the story of Joshua and his mission from the Lord to bring the Israelites to the Promised Land. It was a daunting assignment, for the Jews are known to be a very stubborn and rebellious people, so that even the great Moses failed to bring them to the Promised Land. The faith of Joshua had to be equal to the task or he would surely fail.

Knowing the difficulties Joshua faced to lead the Israelites, the Lord specifically commanded Joshua to meditate on the Word of God day and night to strongly build his faith. It meant to whisper/mutter/ponder the Word of God every chance he could find. Joshua 1:8 says, "The book of the law shall not depart out of thy mouth; but thou shalt meditate therein day and night." The secret of Joshua's power is worth repeating: he had meditated on God's Word often so that the Word of God had taken deep root in his spirit. It was impossible for Joshua at this point in his life to disbelieve the Word of God.

Have we ever considered what would happen if we started believing God's Word without wavering and just rested on God's divine promises? Without doubting the Word of God, we could do great things for God. We limit God with our doubtful minds. The Lord keeps telling us to have faith in Him. The Bible says, "Have faith in God." We need to pay clear attention to what our Lord God is telling us in order to be strong overcomers. Isaiah 26:3 says, "You will keep him in perfect peace whose mind is stayed on Thee."

We are saved by faith, and we continue to move forward in life with us relying and resting on God's Word. The Word of God acts as a sword against the forces of darkness. No power in hell can equal the power of the awesome Word of God. It is so lethal to the devil. The strong spirits of depression and fear cannot withstand the Word of God and have no option but to flee. It is good to be reminded often that the Lord decisively defeated the devil in the wilderness with the sword of the Spirit, the Word of God. It is important to remember to continue with our meditation and not rest until the devil and his demons flee.

Jesus, by choosing to become a man, subjected himself to all kinds of temptations and deceptions of the devil. Jesus knew the power of the Word of God to defeat the devil, and He showed us how to use it. He said boldly in John 14:12, "Greater things you will do ..." We will if we grow in our faith as we learn to believe His Word. Our Lord did not complicate His instructions so that we cannot understand it. His instructions are simple enough that even a young person can understand it well.

All we need to do is develop a childlike faith through our constant meditation, and we will be victorious in life. The sky is the limit, and it is, as far as our faith will bring us. Developing a consistent prayer life will greatly add to our faith. The more we spend quality time with the Lord, the greater our capacity to grow in our faith. Don't we want to spend time with the One we love? Jesus has shown us how to commune with His Father with much fellowship and oneness.

We could truly learn from the example of Lord and do what He practiced. How can we say we loved the Lord when we hardly spend quality time with Him? Perfunctory kind of prayers will not bring us closer to God. Our earnest prayers are like a radio station that connect us with God. A prayerful person is in tune with God and submissive to His will. There are prayers that do not do much to expand our relationship with God. They are those kinds of prayer that center more on what we want God to do for us. Those kinds of prayer won't register well with God. Our prayer life, if is to get the attention of God, is having to empty ourselves and be lost in our worship. It is honoring and worshipping God for who He is. The motive of our hearts must be right, or we will just be wasting our time without getting many results.

Knowing full well the testing and trials we face in life, our God gave us His precious Word to help us navigate through many difficulties in our earthly journey. If we will not easily quit but continue with our study, prayer, and meditation, our faith will continue to grow. What is the purpose of the Bible if it cannot help us in life? Why spend considerable time studying and meditating on the Word of God if it doesn't do us any good?

Our God is a practical God. He is the God of purpose and design. God knows the many challenges we are confronted with while living in this challenging world, and He provides for us the necessary and adequate power and authority to overcome them. The Bible is full of instructions on how to live in this world victoriously.

Our number one enemy, the devil, will try his best to undermine all our efforts to live a godly life. However, while there are strong oppositions coming from the devil and his demons, we also have the powerful antidote against their wicked devices. By learning and doing the instructions God has given to us, we will nullify the attacks of the devil. The world is getting more dangerous, and we need to fortify our spirits.

If perchance we have been meditating for quite a while, and we still haven't experienced a breakthrough, it means we need to have more patience. The spirits of fear and depression are fighting hard to remain a stronghold in our minds, and we need to keep up with our meditation. We should not be discouraged, and when we stay with our meditation, we will surely have our breakthrough. We need to encourage ourselves that we are one more day closer to victory.

Those who understand and practice spiritual authority are free from the relentless probing and attacks of the devil. Occasionally, the devil will send his demons to check our spiritual condition. They are looking for openings and weaknesses that they can easily exploit. We must settle in our minds that the Word of God is powerful and lethal to the devil. When the Word of God is deeply rooted and fully established in our spirits, it becomes overwhelming firepower against the devil. The devil simply cannot win.

The spiritual force comes from the Word of God. The aim of this book is to encourage believers to study and meditate on the Word of God to make them spiritually powerful, useful to God, and being victorious in life. Only believers with strong faith can enjoy and experience wonderful Christian life. These believers are those that God can use to channel His many wonderful blessings and power. Meditation on the Word of God helps fix many problems in our lives. Defeating the spirits of fear and depression is an example of it. The Bible has 365 verses telling us to "Fear not." This should tell us that the devil strongly uses fear to try to destroy us. That is one verse for each day of the year. We need to keep meditating and staying in the Word until we have a breakthrough. Patience is necessary to build godly character. God wants us to develop our godly patience.

Whispering the Word of God slowly and deliberately is like masticating and savoring a delicious morsel of food. It is as if we have been served with an expensive French dish that we need to taste well and remember the experience. Likewise, meditating is not just whispering the Word of God, but pondering and taking in what we are meditating on again and again. The Word of God so nourishes our spirit that our spirits become like well-watered plants.

X. Becoming An Overcomer

Our meditation must be a bold, disciplined, day-to-day habit, not limited and whimsical. We must have tunnel vision of wanting to serve the Lord in order to grow exponentially in our spirits. We must keep pressing onto the high calling of God intended for us. We must plan to win in life. Romans 4:20, 21 says, "He staggered not at the promises of God through unbelief; but was strong in faith, giving glory to God. And being fully persuaded that what he had promised, he was able also to perform." God has planted a seed of greatness in each one of us, and it can only be realized by developing our spirit through our meditation of the Word of God. Romans 4:16 says, "... who quicken the dead, and calling those things which be not as though they were."

Living in victory becomes a reality as we learn how to meditate. The devil is a defeated foe, and we don't need to put up with him. It is our godly inheritance and covenant with God to be strong overcomers. God wants us to pray constantly and thank Him for all the training and blessings we receive daily. God carries us, and we are totally dependent on Him. We are nothing without Christ.

In Matthew 8:5–10, we read about the centurion of great faith. Here, the centurion had the audacity to have a kind of faith that didn't limit God. Be encouraged to believe God's Word and have a living faith. God's perfect love already lives inside us. We receive this love the same way we receive every other promise of His Word, by faith.

The perfect love of God will be manifested in our lives to the exact degree we surrender our lives to the Holy Spirit. He is residing in us and allowing Him to live His life through us is trusting completely in Him. Love is always stronger than fear. Love is the key to a strong faith in overcoming fear. Be reminded again and again of this passage in 1 John 4;18 "perfect love cast out fear ..." If we truly believe God loves us, what is there to fear?

It is as our heart goes out to the needy one with deep compassion that the Lord manifests His presence. Galatians 5:6 tells of us "faith which works through love." Being a Good Samaritan is so pleasing to God. Whenever we go out to help someone, we must pray against any counterattack from the devil, who hates to see us helping and praying for others. We will surely become more skillful as we continue to grow in our God given authority. We must continue to be filled with the Holy Spirit to meet the condition before us. Faith justifies us to righteousness. We must learn to keep decreasing, so Christ can continue to increase in us.

How do we face the many challenges? We face them through His Name, through faith in His Name, and through faith that is by Him. Can God heal us from our afflictions? Healing is the smallest of the gifts; it is but a drop in the bucket in view of what God has stored up for His children. Jeremiah 1:12 says, "for I will hasten my word to perform it." If we want to be big in life, to be fulfilled, and to experience the peace of God, then we need to commit to our close relationship with our heavenly Father and the Lord Jesus Christ, meditate on the Word, and maintain close consultation with the Holy Spirit. With it, we can joyously sing, "All is well, all is well with my soul."

It is so important that we learn to listen to God. Listening to God is fundamental in growing in our faith. God keeps speaking to us through His Word. Throughout the Bible, the Lord keeps giving us comfort, encouragement, and assurances of His divine intervention, love, and godly concern. God is saying to us, "It's OK; I will see you through. Relax in my presence. I will never leave you. My words are for you. Trust me with childlike faith. I will not fail you; I will surely catch you. Learn of me. I have fixed My eyes on you. My plans are to bless you and not to harm you but to give you hope and a future. You're so precious to me. You are mine, and I will always be there for you. There is nothing I cannot do. I am everything that you need. All things are possible with me. My greatest desire is to see you come in a place of complete trust in me."

Our journey in life is not about having great accomplishments or big ministries but a destination of godly character. God wants us to stay close to Him and to trust Him to get us there where He wants us to be. Our experience in sailing on choppy waters is nothing to God. There is nothing that He cannot do. He is in total control in every situation. We are not to lean on our own understanding when difficulties arise but to lean on Him, and He will direct our path. We need to learn how to be still in the presence of the Almighty God. We need to lift up our eyes to our provider, healer, and sustainer.

Names of our Father God

> Jehovah-Jireh (The Lord will provide)—Genesis 22:14
> Jehovah-Nissi (The Lord my Banner)—Exodus 17:15
> Jehovah-Raphe (The Lord my Healer)—Exodus 15:26
> Jehovah-Shalom (My Lord my Peace)—Judges 6:24
> Jehovah Tsidkenu (The Lord my Righteousness)—Jeremiah 23:6
> Jehovah-Raah (The Lord my Shepherd)—Psalm 23:1
> Jehovah-Shammah (The Lord is there; The Lord is enough)—Ezekiel 48:35

Faith always rests. Faith laughs at impossibilities. When we think our faith has been used up, our marvelous and gracious Lord adds to our faith to get it done. As the Spirit of God prays through us, we will find that God will grant the desires of our hearts. We will never get anywhere unless we are in constant pursuit of the power of God. First John 2:14 says, "... the Word of God abide in you, and you've overcome the wicked one." If our God said His Word is true, then it is true.

Christ has won the victory, and His victory is our victory. We can do nothing of ourselves, but the Holy One in us will win the victory. Whatever difficulties we are facing in life, there are passages in the Bible to help us. We meditate on those passages until they get into our spirits. Daniel 11:32 says, "But people who know their God shall prove themselves strong and do great exploits."

Names of the Son, Jesus Christ

> Almighty—Revelation 1:8
> Author and Finisher of our faith—Hebrews 12:2
> Bread of Life—John 6:35
> Captain of Salvation–Hebrews 2:10
> Creator—John 1:3

Good Shepherd—John 10:11
Immanuel—Isaiah 7:14
Lamb of God—John 1:29
Light of the World—John 8:12
True Vine—John 1:9

Again, there is a seed of greatness planted in our spirits. We just need to keep watering and cultivating our spirits with the precious Word of God to cultivate the seed of greatness. We do it until the seed starts to grow and bears fruit. It is a challenge for us to find out our true calling in life. Philippians 1:6 says, "Being confident of this very thing, that he which hath begun a good work in you will perform it until the day of Jesus Christ."

Every trial is a blessing if we view it correctly. Each trial must be viewed and received as an opportunity for us to grow our spiritual muscles. We need to learn to use the sword of the Spirit, the Word of God, masterfully against the wicked spirit. What is the use of having a powerful sword if we don't use it against our nemesis, the devil? Be bold against our enemy who keeps threatening us, our friends, and our families. Proverbs 28:1 says, "The righteous are bold as a lion."

Now that we have read this book, the devil will now try his best to blur our minds from receiving the vital instructions given from the Bible to study and meditate. What we need to do is ask the Holy Spirit to help us apply the biblical principles we have just learned from reading this book. Read it again and again until we become fully convinced of the need to study and meditate. Share this knowledge with friends and loved ones who also need this vital knowledge.

The Word of God is our powerful offensive weapon. It is an awesome gift of God to us. Value it and learn to use it well through our meditation. Christ has the surpassing victory—a victory that is greater than any victory that the world has ever known, and He will guide us, as we learn to navigate through His Word. It is a blessed thing to learn that the Word of God can never fail. The study and meditation will lead us to a peaceful and fulfilling life. It is our great inheritance.

X. Becoming An Overcomer

When we fortify our spirits with the Word of God, we can truly enjoy wholesome and powerful living.

We can live in the power of His might, free from fear and depression. Acts 19:20 says, "So mightily grew the Word and prevailed." All God expects us to do is to do our best, and He will do the rest. God wants us to enlarge and expand our steps. Jeremiah 33:3 says, "Call unto me and I will answer thee, and show thee great and mighty things, which thou know not." Yield to the Word of God, and it will be the greatest adventure of our lives. It will be the most fulfilling life for us. Take up the challenge of meditating on God's awesome Word and be the best we can be for God. The sky is the limit for us.

HOW TO PRAY TO RECEIVE OUR LORD JESUS CHRIST INTO OUR HEARTS:

Before we can access the power of God's Word, we must first become a genuine child of God. We first need to repent of our sins and receive (commit) Jesus Christ into our hearts. It is a holy covenant between God and us. If we have decided to give our whole heart to Jesus, then we can follow these steps. In doing so, we will become a member of God's royal family. The power of God's Word becomes activated in our spirits, and it will be at our disposal as we grow in our faith. The Word of God is now our guide in our day-to-day earthly journey. Here are the steps to follow to receive Jesus Christ as our Lord and Savior:

1. *All HAVE SINNED.* We need to confess and repent of our sin. Romans 3:23 declares, "For all have sinned, and come short of the glory of God" Romans 6:23 says, "For the wages of sin is (spiritual) death; but the gift of God is eternal life through Christ Jesus."
2. *JUDGEMENT AFTER DEATH.* "Hebrews 9:27 states, "It is appointed unto man once to die, after that judgment." There is no purgatory or second chance.
3. *SALVATION IS A GIFT AND NOT OF GOOD WORK.* Ephesians 2:8, 9 says, "For by grace are ye saved through faith; and that not

of yourselves, it is a gift of God. Not of works, lest any man should boast." Salvation is a free gift from God. We can't earn it or work for it by trying to be good. It's a gift.
4. *JESUS CHRIST HAS ALREADY PAID FOR OUR SIN.* Jesus died at the Cross to pay for your sin. Romans 5:8 says, "... while we were sinners, Christ died for us."
5. *WE NEED A SAVIOR.* First Timothy 1:1 tells us that, "... Lord Jesus Christ, which is our hope." Colossians 1:27 says, "... Christ in you, the hope of glory." Our faith in Jesus Christ, not our good work, will save us. It is putting our whole trust in Christ.
6. *WE NEED TO RECEIVE CHRIST INTO OUR HEART.* John 1:12 says, "But as many as received Him, to them gave the power to become the sons of God." John 3:16 says, "For God so loved the world that He gave His only begotten Son, that whosoever believeth (committed) in Him, should not perish but have everlasting life."
7. *PRAY NOW TO RECEIVE CHRIST IN YOUR HEART.* This is the most important decision you will ever make in your life. You need to open your heart to Jesus. Wholeheartedly confess and repent of your sins and receive (commit) the Lord into your heart. Give your heart to Him and promise to follow Him all the rest of your life. If this is the prayer of your heart, you are now a new creature in Christ. Second Corinthians 5:17 states, "Therefore if any man be in Christ, he is a new creature; old things are passed away, all things become new."
8. *FIND A FELLOWSHIP THAT PREACHES SOUND TEACHINGS OF THE BIBLE.* Ask the Holy Spirit to guide you to find the right fellowship. You need to fellowship with other fellow believers to guide you in your walk with Christ.

OUR GUIDE TO OUR DAILY BIBLE READING:

Make it our goal to read one to two chapters of the New Testament daily, and read the Old Testament later on. Ask the Holy Spirit to guide us every time we read the Bible. Start from the Book of Matthew, one chapter at a time, in consecutive order. Underline key passages in each chapter. If we are beginners, reading the Bible for the first time, it won't make much sense to us, but in time, it will become clear to us.

Buy yourselves the New Testament Bible, King James version, from the National Publishing Company. It is a handy book to study and being sold at a discounted price. You also need to buy a Bible with the old and new testament with a concordance. Add to it a good Bible commentary. As a beginner, you will want to stay with the New Testament initially. There are many books on how to study the Bible that will help you in our study. You could also avail yourself of many Bible teachers found in the website; but be careful to avoid the teachings of the cults. The cults will always minimize Jesus Christ and deny His Deity. We need to join a good Bible study group to accelerate our understanding of the Bible.

Studying the Word of God is a wonderful journey. It will be so refreshing to your spirit to learn the Word of God. The more you study it, the more it will become relevant to your spiritual life. Prepare to receive many blessings in life as you grow in the Word of God. It is truly life-changing. It will guide you to the best pathway to travel in life. The Word of God will protect you from many pitfalls along the way. Psalm 119:105 says, "Thy Word is a lamp unto my feet, and a light unto my path."

WORD OF GOD TO MEDITATE ON:

WORD OF GOD

Romans 10:17, "So then faith cometh by hearing and hearing, by the word of God."

Psalm 119:130, "The entrance of the words giveth light; it giveth understanding to the simple."

Psalm 119:105, "Thy word is a lamp unto my feet, and a light unto my path."

1 Peter 2:2,"As a newborn babe, desire the sincere milk of the word, that ye may grow thereby."

1 Peter 1:23, "Being born again, not of corruptible seed, but of incorruptible, by the word of God, which live and abide forever."

Joshua 1:8, "This book of the law shall not depart out of thy mouth, but thou shalt meditate therein day and night, that thou may observe to do according to all that is written therein; for then thou shalt make thy way prosperous, and then thou shalt have good success."

Deut.11:18, "Therefore shall ye lay up my words in your heart and in your soul, and bind them for a sign upon your hand, that they may be as frontlets between your eyes."

SEEKING GOD

Hebrews 11:6, "But without faith it is impossible to please God; for he that cometh to God must believe that He is, and that He is a rewarder of them that diligently seek Him."

Deuteronomy 4:29, "But if from thence thou shalt seek the Lord thy God, thou shalt find him, if thou seek Him with all thy heart and with all thy soul."

Ezra 8:22, "... the hand of our God is upon all them that seek Him; but his power and His wrath is against all them that forsake Him."

Lamentations 3:25, "The Lord is good unto them that wait for Him, to the soul that seek Him."

2 Chronicles 15:2, "... The Lord is with you, while ye be with Him, and if you seek Him, He will be found of you; but if ye forsake Him, He will forsake you."

X. Becoming An Overcomer

ETERNAL LIFE

1 John 2:25, "And this is the promise that He hath promised us, even eternal life."

1 John 1:25, 26, "Jesus said unto her, I am the resurrection and the life; he that believeth in me, though he were dead, yet shall he live. And whosoever live and believeth in me shall never die. Believe thou this?"

1 John 5:13, "These things have I written unto you that believe on the name of the Son of God; that ye may know that ye have eternal life, and that ye may believe on the name of the Son of God."

Revelation 21:4, "And God shall wipe away all tears from their eyes; and there shall be no more death, neither sorrow, nor crying, neither shall there be any more pain; for the former things are passed away."

Romans 6:23, "For the wages of sin is death; but the gift of God is eternal life through Jesus Christ our Lord."

PEACE

Philippians 4:7, "And the peace of God, which pass all understanding, shall keep your hearts and minds through Christ Jesus."

Psalm 85:8, "I will hear what God the Lord will speak, for he will speak peace unto his people, and to his saints."

2 Thessalonians 3:16, "Now the Lord of peace himself give you peace always by all means."

John 14:27, "Peace I leave with you, my peace I give unto you; not as the world giveth, give I unto you. Let not your heart be troubled, neither let it be afraid."

Colossians 3:15, "And let the peace of God rule in your hearts, to which also ye are called in one body; and be ye thankful."

MEDITATION

Joshua 1:8, "This book of the law shall not depart out of the mouth but thou shalt meditate therein day and night, that thou may observe to do according to all that is written therein; for then thou shalt make thy way prosperous, and thou shalt have good success."

Psalm 1:2, "But his delight is in law of the Lord; and in his law doth he meditates day and night."

Psalm 119:15, 16, "I will meditate in thy precepts, and have respect unto thy ways. I will delight myself in thy statutes; I will not forget thy word."

Psalm 19:14, "Let the words of my mouth, and the meditation of my heart, be acceptable in thy sight, O Lord, my strength, and my redeemer."

Psalm 104:34, "My meditation of him shall be sweet; I will be glad in the Lord."

Psalm 119:97,"O how love I thy law! It is my meditation all the day."

Psalm 119:103, "How sweet are thy words unto my taste! yea, sweeter than honey to my mouth!"

POWER OF THE WORD

Hebrews 4:12, "For the word of God is quick and powerful, and sharper than a two edged sword ..."

Hebrews 4:2, "... but the word preached did not profit them, not being mixed with faith in them that heard it."

John 11:40, "... if thou would believe, thou should see the glory of God."

2 Timothy 3:16, "All scripture is given by inspiration of God, and is profitable for doctrine, for reproof, for correction, for instruction in righteousness."

Acts 20:32, "And now, brethren, I command you to God, and to the word of His grace, which is able to build you up..."

Proverbs 6:23,"For the commandments is a lamp; and the law is light, and reproofs of instructions are the way of life."

PATIENCE

Galatians 6:9, "Let us not be weary in well doing; for in due season we shall reap, if we faint not."

Matthew 24:13, "But he that shall endure unto the end, he same shall be saved."

Hebrews 6:12, "That ye be not slothful, but followers of them who through faith and patience inherit the promises."

James 1:2–4, "My brethren, count it all joy when ye fall into divers temptations; knowing this, that the trying of your faith work patience. But let patience have her perfect work, that ye may be perfect and entire, wanting nothing."

Romans 5:2, 4, "And not only so, but we glory in tribulations also; knowing that tribulation work patience, and patience, experience and experience, hope."

1 Peter 2:20, "For what glory is it, if, when we be buffeted for your faults, ye shall take it patiently? but if, when ye do well, and suffer for it, ye take it patiently, this is acceptable to God."

ABIDE

John 15:4, "Abide in me and I in you. As the branch cannot bear fruit of itself, except it abides in the vine; no more can ye, except ye abide in me."

John 15:6, "If a man abides not in me, he is cast forth as a branch, and is withered, and men gather them, and cast them into the fire, and they are burned."

John 15:10, "If ye keep my commandments, ye shall abide in my love; even as I have kept my Father's commandments, and abide in his love."

1 Peter 1:23, "Being born again, not of corruptible seed, but of incorruptible, by the word of God, which live and abide forever."

1 John 2:14, "... and the word of God abide in you, and ye have overcome the wicked one."

1 John 2:17, "... but he that doeth the will of God abide forever."

1 John 3:6, "Whosoever abide in him sin not ..."

FAITH

Hebrews 11:1, "Now faith is the substance of things hoped for, the evidence of things not seen."

Hebrews 11:6, "... he that cometh to God must believe that he is, and that he is a rewarder of them that diligently seek him."

Ephesians 2:8, "For by grace are ye saved through faith; and that not of yourselves; it is the gift of God."

Galatians 3:26, "For ye are all the children of God by faith in Christ Jesus."

1 Corinthians 16:13, "Watch ye, stand fast in the faith, quit you like men, be strong."

2 Corinthians 5:7, "For we walk by faith, not by sight."

Ephesians 3:17–19, "That Christ may dwell in your hearts by faith; that ye, being rooted and grounded in love, may be able to comprehend with all saints what is the breadth, and length, and depth, and height; and to know the love of Christ, which pass knowledge, that ye might be filled with all the fullness of God."

Hebrews 12:2, "Looking unto Jesus the author and finisher of our faith; who for the joy that was set before him endured the cross, despising the shame, and is set down at the right of the throne of God."

FEAR

Mark 4:40,"And he said unto them, why are ye so fearful? How is it that ye have no faith?"

Isaiah 41:13, "for I the Lord thy God will hold thy right hand, saying unto thee, fear not; I will help thee."

Proverbs 1:33, "But whoso hearken unto me shall dwell safely, and shall be quiet down from fear of evil."

Proverbs 3:25, 26, "Be not afraid of sudden fear, neither of the desolation of the wicked, when it cometh. For the Lord shall be thy confidence, and shall keep thy foot from being taken."

2 Timothy 1:7, "For God hath not given us the spirit of fear, but of power, of love and of sound mind."

Proverbs 3:24,"When thou lie down, thou shalt not be afraid; yea, thou shalt lie down, and thy sleep shall be sweet."

Isaiah 54:14, "In righteousness shalt thou be established; thou shalt be far from oppression; for thou shalt not fear, and from terror, for it shall come near thee."

Romans 8:15, "For ye have not received the spirit of bondage again to fear; but ye have received the Spirit of adoption, whereby we cry, Abba Father."

Hebrews 13:6, "So that we may boldly say, the Lord is my helper, and I will not fear what man shall do unto me."

John 14:27,"Peace I leave with you, my peace I give unto you, not as the world giveth, give I unto you. Let not your heart be troubled, neither let it be afraid."

Psalm 27:1, "The Lord is my light and my salvation; whom shall I fear? The Lord is the strength of my life, of whom shall I be afraid."

BELIEF:

John 1:12, "But as many as received him, to them gave he power to become the sons of God, even to them believe on his name."

John 3:18, "He that believeth on him is not condemned; but he that believeth not is condemned already, because he hath not believed in the name of the only begotten Son of God."

John 3:36,"He that believeth on the Son hath everlasting life; and he that believeth not the Son shall not see life, but the wrath of God abides in him."

John 12:46, "I am come a light unto the world, that whosoever believeth on me should not abide in darkness."

John 6:35, "And Jesus said unto them, I am the bread of life; he that cometh to me shall never hunger; and he that believeth on me shall never thirst."

Mark 9:23, "Jesus said unto him, if thou canst believe, all things are possible to him that believeth."

John 6:47, "Verily, verily, I say unto you, he that believeth in me hath everlasting life."

CHARITY:

Ecclesiastes 11:1, "Cast thy bread upon the waters, for thou shalt find it after many days."

Proverbs 22:9,"He hath bountiful eye shall be blessed; for he giveth of his bread to the poor."

Proverbs 28:27, "He that giveth unto the poor shall not lack, but he that hide his eyes shall have many a curse."

2 Corinthians 9:7, "Every man according as he purposes in his heart, so let him give; not grudgingly, or of necessity, for God love a cheerful giver."

Psalm 37:25, 26, "I have been young, and now am old; yet have I not seen the righteous forsaken, nor his seed begging for bread. He is ever merciful, and lend, and his seed is blessed."

1 Timothy 6:17,18, "Charge them that are rich in this world, that they be not high mind, nor trust in uncertain riches, but in the living God, who giveth us richly all things to enjoy. That they do good, that they be rich in good works, ready to distribute, willing to communicate."

Matthew 25:40, "And the King shall answer and say unto them, verily I say unto you, inasmuch as ye have done it unto one of the least of these my brethren, ye has done it unto me."

COMFORT

Psalm 138:7, "Though I walk in the midst of trouble, thou wilt revive me, thou shalt stretch forth thine hand against the wrath of mine enemies, and thy right hand shall save me."

Psalm 18:2, "The Lord is my rock, and my fortress, and my deliverer; my God, my strength, in whom I will trust; my buckler, and the horn of my salvation, and my high tower."

Psalm 22:24, "For he hath not despised nor abhorred the affliction of the afflicted; neither hath he hid his face from him, but when he cried unto him, he heard."

Psalm 37:24, "Though he falls, he shall not be utterly cast down; for the Lord uphold him with his hand."

Nahum 1:7, "The Lord is good, a strong hold on the day of trouble; and he know them that trust in him."

Psalm 37:39, "But the salvation of the righteous is of the Lord; he is their strength in the time of trouble."

Psalm 55:22, "Cast thy burden upon the Lord, and he shall sustain thee, he shall never suffer the righteous to be moved."

Psalm 9:9, "The Lord also will be a refuge for the oppressed, a refuge in times of trouble."

Psalm 27:14, "Wait on the Lord, be of good courage, and he shall strengthen thine heart, wait I say, on the Lord."

CONTENTMENT:

Proverbs 17:22, "A merry heart doeth good like a medicine; but a broken spirit dried the bones."

X. Becoming An Overcomer

Proverbs 15:15, "All the days of the afflicted are evil; but he that is of a merry heart hath a continual feast."

Proverbs 4:30, "A sound heart is the life of the flesh; but envy the rottenness of the bones."

1 Timothy 6:6, "But godliness with contentment is great gain."

Proverbs 23:17, 18, "Let not thine heart envy sinners, but be thou in the fear of the Lord all the day long. For surely there is an end, and thine expectation shall not be cut off."

COURAGE

Psalm 27:14, "Wait on the Lord, be of good courage, and he shall strengthen thine heart; wait I say, on the Lord."

Psalm 37:28, "For the Lord love judgment, and forsake not his saints; they are preserved forever, but the seed of the wicked shall be cut off."

Isaiah 43:1, "But now thus says the Lord that created thee, O Jacob, and he that formed thee, O Israel, fear not. For I have redeemed thee, I have called thee by thy name; thou art mine."

2 Kings 6:16, "... fear not, for they that be wish us are more than they that be with them."

Psalm 37:3, "Trust in the Lord, and do good, so shalt thou dwell in the land, and verily thou shalt be fed."

Isaiah 40:29, "He giveth power to the faint; and to them that have no might he increases their strength."

Psalm 31:24, "Be of good courage, and he shall strengthen your heart, all ye that hope in the Lord."

Philippians 4:12, 13, "I know both how to be abased, and I know how to be abound; everywhere and in all things I am instructed both to be full and to be hungry, both to abound and to suffer need. I can do all things through Christ which strengthened me."

FAITHFULNESS:

Deuteronomy 7:9, "Know therefore that the lord thy God, he is good, the faithful God, which keep covenant and mercy with them that love him and keep his commandments into a thousand generations."

Deuteronomy 4:31, "For the Lord thy God is a merciful God; he will not forsake thee, neither destroy thee, nor forget the covenant of thy fathers which he swore unto them."

Psalm 103:8, "He hath remembered his covenant forever, the word which he commanded to a thousand generations."

Numbers 23:19, "God is not a man, that he should lie; neither the son of man, that he should repent, hath he said and shall he not do it? Hath he spoken, and shall he not make it good."

Hebrews 10:23, "Let us hold fast the profession (confession) of our faith without wavering; for he is faithful that promised."

2 Timothy 2:13, "If we believe not, yet he abides faithful, he cannot deny himself."

Psalm 9:10, "And they that know thy name will put their trust in thee; for thou, Lord, hast not forsaken them that seek thee."

Psalm 119:89, 90, "Forever, O Lord, thy word is settled in heaven. Thy faithfulness is unto all generations."

2 Corinthians 1:20, "For all the promises of God in him are yea, and in him Amen, unto the glory of God by us."

Psalm 89:34, "My covenant will I not break, nor after the thing that is gone out of my lips."

Isaiah 54:10, "For the mountains shall depart and the hills be removed, but my kindness shall not depart from thee, neither shall the covenant of my peace be removed, says the Lord that hath mercy on thee."

Isaiah 46:11, "… yea, I have spoken it, I will also bring it to pass; I have purposed it, I will also do it."

FORGIVENESS

Mark 11:25, 26, "And when ye stand praying, forgive, if ye have fought against any; that your Father also which is in heaven may forgive you your trespasses. But if ye do not forgive, neither will your Father which is in heaven forgive your trespasses."

Matthew 6:14, "But if you forgive men of their trespasses, your heavenly Father will also forgive you."

Romans 12:20, "Therefore if thine enemy hunger, feed him, if he thirsts, give him drink …"

Luke 6:35–38, "But love ye your enemies, and do good, and lend, hoping for nothing again; and your reward shall be great, and ye shall be the children of the Highest; for he is kind unto unthankful and to the evil. Be ye therefore merciful, as your Father also is merciful. Judge not, and ye shall not be judged, condemn not and ye shall not be condemned, forgive and ye shall be forgiven."

Proverbs 20:23, "Say not thou, I will recompense evil; but wait on the Lord, and he shall save thee."

FRUITFULNESS

Psalm 1:3, "And he shall be like a tree planted by the rivers of water, that bringeth forth his fruit in his season; his leaf also shall not wither, and whatsoever he doeth shall prosper."

Jeremiah 31:12, "Therefore they shall come and sing in the heights of Zion, and shall flow together to the goodness of the Lord, for wheat, and for wine, and for oil, and for the young of the flock and of the herd, and their soul shall be as watered garden; and they shall not sorrow more at all."

Psalm 92:14, "They shall bring forth fruit in old age; they shall be fat and flourishing."

2 Peter 1:8, "I will be as the dew unto Israel; he shall grow as the lily, and cast forth his roots as Lebanon."

GUIDANCE

Psalm 48:14, "For this God is our God for ever and ever; he will be our guide even upon death."

Proverbs 16:9, "A man's heart devises his way; but the Lord direct his steps."

Isaiah 28:26, "For his God doth instruct him to discretion, and doth teach him."

Proverbs 11:5, "The righteous of the perfect shall direct his way; but the wicked shall fall by his own wickedness."

Proverbs 3:6, "In all thy ways acknowledge him, and he shall direct thy paths."

Isaiah 42:16, "And I will bring the blind by a way that they knew not; I will lead them in the paths that they have not known, I will make darkness light before them, and crooked things straight. These things will I do unto them, and not forsake them."

Psalm 32:8, "I will instruct thee and teach thee in the way which thou shalt go; I will guide thee with mine eye."

Psalm 73:24, "Thou shalt guide me with thy counsel, and afterward receive me to glory."

X. Becoming An Overcomer

GUILT

1 John 1:9, "If we confess our sins, he is faithful and just to forgive us our sins, and to cleanse us from all unrighteousness."

Isaiah 55:7, "Let the wicked forsake his way, and the unrighteous man his thoughts; and let him return unto the Lord, and he will have mercy upon him; and our God, for he will abundantly pardon."

2 Chronicles 30:9, "For the Lord your God is gracious and merciful, and will not turn away his face from you, if ye return unto him."

Psalm 103:12, "As far as the east is from the west, so far hath he removed our transgressions from us."

Hebrews 8:12, "For I will be merciful to their unrighteousness, and their sins and their iniquities will I remember no more."

2 Corinthians 5:17, "Therefore if any man be in Christ, he is a new creature; old things are passed away, behold, all things are become new.'

DIVINE HELP

Psalm 37:39, "But the salvation of the righteous is of the Lord. He is their strength in the time of trouble."

Psalm 146:8, "The Lord is good, a strong hold in the day of trouble; and he knows them that trust in him."

Psalm 37:24, "Though he falls, he shall not be utterly cast down; for the Lord uphold him with his hand."

Psalm 32:7, "Thou art my hiding place; thou shalt preserve me from trouble; thou shalt compass me about with songs and deliverance."

Psalm 42:11, "Why art thou cast down, O my soul? and why art thou disquieted within me? Hope thou in God; for I shall yet praise him, who is the health of my countenance, and my God."

Psalm 91:10, 11, "There shall be no evil befall thee, neither shall any plaque come nigh thy dwelling. For he shall give his angels charge over thee, to keep thee in all thy ways."

Psalm 9:9, "He shall deliver thee in six troubles; yea, in seven there shall no evil touch you."

Psalm 34:19, "Many are the afflictions of the righteous; but the Lord delivered him out of them all."

HOLY SPIRIT

Proverbs 1:23, "... behold, I will pour out my spirit unto you, I will make known my words unto you."

John 14:16, 17, "And I will pray the Father, and he shall give you another Comforter, that he may abide with you forever. Even the Spirit of truth, whom the world cannot receive, because it sees him not, neither know him; but ye know him, for he dwells with you and shall be in you."

John 16:13, "Howbeit, when he, the Spirit of truth, is come, he will guide you into all truth; for he shall not speak of himself; but whatsoever he shall hear, that shall he speak; and he will shew your things to come."

Luke 11:13, "If you then, being evil, know how to give good gifts unto your children, how much more shall your heavenly Father give the Holy Spirit to them that ask him."

Ezra 36:27, "And I will put my spirit within you, and cause you to walk in my statutes, and ye shall keep my judgments, and do them."

Romans 8:26,27, "Likewise the Spirit also helps our infirmities; for we know not what we should pray for as we ought, but the Spirit itself make intercession for us with groaning which cannot be uttered. And he that search the hearts know what is the mind of the Spirit, because he makes intercession for the saints according to the will of God."

Romans 14:17, "For the kingdom of God is not meat and drink; but righteousness, and peace, and joy in the Holy Ghost."

1 Corinthians 2:12, "Now we have received not the spirit of the world, but the spirit which is of God, that we might know the things that are freely given to us of God."

Romans 8:15, "For ye have not received the spirit of bondage again to fear; but ye have received the Spirit of adoption, whereby we cry, Abba Father."

HOPE

Psalm 42:11, "Why are thou cast down, O my soul? and why art thou disquieted within me? Hope thou in God; for I shall yet praise him, who is the health of countenance, and my God."

Colossians 1:5, "For the hope which is laid up for you in heaven, whereof ye heard before in the word of the truth of the gospel."

Colossians 1:27, "... which is Christ in you, the hope of glory."

Psalm 31:24, "Be of good courage, and he shall strengthen your heart, all ye that hope in the Lord."

Psalm 71:5, "For thou art my hope, O Lord God; thou art my trust from my youth."

1 Peter 1:3, "Blessed be the God and Father of our Lord Jesus Christ, which according to the abundant mercy hath begotten us again unto a lively hope by the resurrection of Jesus Christ from the dead."

JOY

Psalm 118:15, "The voice of rejoicing and salvation is the tabernacles of the righteous; the right hand of the Lord doeth valiantly.

Psalm 118:13, "Thou hast put gladness in my heart, more than in the time that their corn and their wine increased."

Psalm 126:5, 6, "They that sow in tears shall reap in joy. He that go frothed and wept, bearing precious seed, shall doubtless come again with rejoicing, bringing the sheaves with him."

Psalm 97:11,12, "Light is sown for the righteous, and gladness for the upright in heart Rejoice in the Lord, ye righteous, and give thanks at the remembrance of His holiness."

Hebrews 3:18, "Yet I will rejoice in the Lord, I will joy in the God of my salvation."

Psalm 33:21, "For our heart shall rejoice in him. because we have trusted in his holy name."

Psalm 68:3, "My soul shall be satisfied as with marrow and fatness; and my mouth shall praise thee with joyful lips."

LOVING GOD

Deuteronomy 7:9, "Know therefore that the Lord thy God, he is God, the faithful God, which keep covenant and mercy with them that loves him and keep his commandments to a thousand generations."

Proverbs 8:17, "I love them that love me; and those that seek me early shall find me."

John 14:21, "He that hath my commandments, and keep them, he is that love me; and he that me love me shall be loved of my Father, and I will love him, and I will manifest myself to him."

Proverbs 8:21, "That I may cause those that love me to inherit substance; and I will fill their treasures."

Psalm 37:4, "Delight thyself also in the Lord; and he shall give thee the desires of thine heart."

X. Becoming An Overcomer

Psalm 145:20, "The Lord preserved all them that love him; but all the wicked will be destroy."

Psalm 91:14, "Because he hath set his love upon me, therefore will I deliver him; I will set him on high, because he hath known m name."

1 Corinthians 2:9, "But as it is written, eye hath not seen, nor ear heard, neither have entered into the heart of man, the things which God hath prepared for them that love him."

Ephesians 6:24, "Grace be with all them that love our Lord Jesus Christ in sincerity."

MEEKNESS

Matthew 5:5, "Blessed are the meek, for they shall inherit the earth."

Psalm 22:26, "The meek shall eat and be satisfied; they shall praise the Lord that seek him; your heart shall live forever."

Psalm 149:4, "For the Lord taketh pleasure in his people; he will beautify the meek with salvation."

Psalm 147:6, "The Lord lifted up the meek; he cast the wicked down to the ground."

Zephaniah 2:3, "Seek ye the Lord, all ye meek of the earth, which have wrought his judgment; seek righteousness, seek meekness, it may be ye shall be hid in the day of Lord's anger."

1 Peter 3:4, "But let it be the hidden man of the heart, in that which is not corruptible, even the ornament of a meek and quiet spirit, which in the sight of God of great price."

Psalm 37:11,"But the meek shall inherit the earth; and shall delight themselves in the abundance of peace."

Proverbs 15:1, "A soft answer turn away wrath; but grievous words stir up anger."

GOD'S PROTECTION:

Proverbs 18:10, "The name of the Lord is a strong tower; the righteous run into it, and is safe."

Psalm 121:7, 8, "The Lord shall preserve thee from all evil; he shall preserve thy soul. The Lord shall preserve thy going out and thy going in for this time forth, and even for evermore."

Proverbs 3:24, "When thou lie down, thou shalt not be afraid; yea, thou shalt lie down, and thy sleep shall be sweet."

Psalm 112:7, "He shall not be afraid of evil tidings; his heart is fixed, trusting in the Lord."

Psalm 91:9,10, "Because thou hast made the Lord, which is my refuge, even the Highest God, thy habitation; there shall no evil befall thee, neither shall any plague come nigh thy dwelling."

Ezekiel 34:28, "And they shall no more be a prey to the heathen, neither shall the beast of the land devour them, but they shall dwell safely, and none shall make them afraid."

Proverbs 1:33, "But whoso hearkened unto me shall dwell safely, and shall be quiet from fear of evil."

Psalm 27:1, "The Lord is my light and my salvation; whom shall I fear? The Lord is the strength of my life, of whom shall I be afraid."

Psalm 4:8, "I will both lay me down in peace and sleep, for thou, Lord, only makes me dwell in safety."

RIGHTEOUSNESS

Psalm 84:11, "For the Lord God is a sun and shield; the Lord will give grace and glory, no good things will he withheld from them that walk uprightly."

Psalm 34:10, "The young lions do lack, and suffer hunger; but they that seek the Lord shall not want any good thing."

Proverbs 10:24, "The fear of the wicked, it shall come upon him; but the desire of the righteous shall be granted."

Matthew 6:33, "But seek ye first the kingdom of God, and his righteousness; and all these things shall be added unto thee."

Romans 8:32, "He that spared not his own Son, but delivered him up for us all, how shall he now with him also freely give us all things?

Isaiah 3:10, "Say yes to the righteous, hat it shall be well with him; for they shall eat he fruit of their doings."

Psalm 23:6, "Surely goodness and mercy shall follow me all the days of my life; and I will dwell in the house of the Lord forever."

TRUST

Psalm 46:1, "God is our refuge and strength, a very present help in trouble."

Psalm 84:11, "For the Lord God is a sun and shield; the Lord will give grace and glory; no good thing will he withhold from them that walk uprightly."

Psalm 37:3–5, "Trust in the Lord, and do good; so shalt thou dwell in the land, and verily thou shalt be fed. Delight thyself also in the Lord; and he shall give thee the desires of your heart. Commit thy way unto the lord; trust also in him; and he shall be bringing it to pass."

Proverbs 3:5, 6, "Trust in the Lord with all thine heart; and lean not unto thine own understanding. In all thy ways acknowledge him, and he shall direct thy paths."

Luke 12:32, "Fear not, little flock; for it is your Father's good pleasure to give you the kingdom."

1 Peter 5:7, "Casting all your care upon him; for he cares for you."

Psalm 125:1, "They that trust in the Lord shall be as mount Zion, which cannot be removed, but abide forever."

ENDORSEMENTS:

" Amazing book"....... John W.

" A must reading for believers"....Bert T.

" Book for those those suffering from fear & depression"...Estela D.

" I highly recommend it".........Joy D.

" Many believers around the world would greatly benefit from it".. Ferdie D.

CPSIA information can be obtained
at www.ICGtesting.com
Printed in the USA
FSOW04n0123090216
16717FS